THE NHS TRANSFORMED

THE NHS TRANSFORMED
A GUIDE TO THE HEALTH REFORMS

IAN HOLLIDAY

baseline
BOOKS

First published 1992 by
Baseline Book Company
PO Box 34
Chorlton
Manchester M21 1LL

British Library Cataloguing in Publication Data

ISBN 1 897626 00 2

Cover design   Ian Price
Cover illustration   Min Cooper
Typesettting   Kathryn Holliday
Printed and bound by Nuffield Press, Oxford

ACKNOWLEDGEMENTS

For detailed and insightful comments, I am greatly indebted to Martin Burch, Alison Enticknap and Bruce Wood. They have saved me from many errors of fact and judgment. I bear full responsibility for those which remain. **IH**

CONTENTS

TABLES

ABBREVIATIONS

AHA	Area Health Authority
ASI	Adam Smith Institute
BMA	British Medical Association
CHC	Community Health Council
CCT	Compulsory Competitive Tendering
CPS	Centre for Policy Studies
DHA	District Health Authority
DHSS	Department of Health and Social Security
DMT	District Management Team
DMU	Directly Managed Unit
FHSA	Family Health Services Authority
FPC	Family Practitioner Committee
GDP	Gross Domestic Product
GP	General Practitioner
HMO	Health Maintenance Organisation
IEA	Institute of Economic Affairs
NHS	National Health Service
QALY	Quality-Adjusted Life Year
RAWP	Resource Allocation Working Party
RHA	Regional Health Authority
WHO	World Health Organisation

INTRODUCTION

The National Health Service (NHS) is a much-loved British institution, ranking second only to the monarchy in the nation's affections. Yet, admired and in many ways revered as it might be, the NHS is now subject to a process of fundamental change. The present programme of health reforms, built around the twin concepts of purchasers and providers in an internal market, is the most significant since creation of the NHS itself in the late 1940s. By the late 1990s, it will have resulted in its transformation.

THE REFORM AGENDA

The Conservatives' reform agenda has in fact developed in two main ways. First came a set of managerial reforms, evident in minor initiatives taken at the start of the 1980s, but only pursued with vigour from 1984. These are known as the move to general management, and are responsible for a cultural shift within the NHS from professional ways of working to a more businesslike orientation.

Second, and far more radically, came a set of structural reforms, debated chiefly in 1988 and outlined in 1989, but only introduced from 1991 onwards. These are the internal market reforms which are currently undermining the old egalitarian orientation of the NHS, and replacing it with a more individualistic mode. As these reforms are being introduced in a gradual fashion, this change is happening over a number of years. By the end of the 1990s – possibly earlier – it will be complete.

It is important to note at the outset that the two reform programmes have distinct and in many ways conflicting dynamics. The first introduced a regulatory dynamic into the NHS through institution of a managerial hierarchy which stretches from top to bottom of the organisation. The second, by contrast, is currently doing much to undermine strategic control of the Service. Through fragmentation of the old NHS structure it is increasingly diminishing the possibility of a centrally-directed Service.

The impact of reform is therefore different in the two cases. Although both initiatives are having profound effects on the way in which the NHS operates, only the second set is transforming its basic character. The general management reforms of the 1980s certainly made the NHS more businesslike than was previously the case, but they did not transform its basic structure. By contrast, the internal market reforms of the 1990s, which place the contractual relations of a market at the heart of the NHS, are now operating to fragment its unified character. It is no exaggeration to state that 1991 marks the start of a process whereby the old NHS is gradually being replaced by a new model.

It should, however, be noted that this dramatic change could not have happened had the managerial reforms of the 1980s not already taken place. The NHS used to be an essentially collegiate institution run, to caricature only slightly, by doctors. Its predominant managerial mode was consensus decision making by teams of professionals. The general management reforms of 1984 generated a paradigm shift in NHS internal operations. Out went consensus management by professionals. In came businesslike managerial hierarchies.

This paradigm shift was necessary to the more recent fragmentation of the NHS, which will be the dominant feature of the NHS in the 1990s. Unless a cultural shift towards business practices had taken place in the 1980s, an internal market necessarily based on a contract culture – rather than on the old professional culture of mutual trust – would not have worked and could not therefore have been introduced.

The two elements of the Conservatives' reform agenda have, then, elements of both compatibility and tension. The internal market programme both builds on and in an important sense undermines the drive to general management. When the Thatcher administration undertook to break the NHS into small units, it certainly reinforced business practices, but it also embarked on a programme of radical reform which in many ways undercut its earlier managerial initiative. Without that earlier initiative the move to a new model NHS could not, however, have been made.

In the event, implementation of the Conservatives' internal market reforms did not commence until after Margaret Thatcher's fall from power. NHS reform continues to be pursued with vigour by the Major administration.

SCOPE AND LIMITS OF REFORM

In the midst of a programme of radical reform, it is important to state what has not changed – and what will not change, at least in the foreseeable future – in the NHS. Two of the Service's defining principles – that it be predominantly tax-funded and mainly free at the point of use – are virtually untouched by reform. Although there has been some chipping away at the edges of these principles – in, for example, the substantial increase in charges witnessed in the 1980s – neither is under serious threat.

What is being created in the 1990s is, therefore, a new NHS. It is not a system of health care which rests on wholly different principles from those which have until now defined the NHS. Were the two key principles of tax funding and free health care at the point of use to come under serious threat, it would be difficult to hold that the NHS continued to exist in any meaningful form. There are – to repeat – no current or foreseeable moves in this direction.

STRUCTURE OF ARGUMENT

This book analyses the NHS reforms which have been pursued since the early 1980s, and the emergence of a new NHS which has been happening only since 1991.

Its first four chapters investigate the old NHS. They look in particular at its creation at the end of World War Two, at its subsequent development, and at its standing in an international context. The first element of the Conservatives' reform programme – the paradigm shift to general management – is investigated here.

The next three chapters analyse the new NHS. They look first at the internal market reforms which are responsible for transformation of the NHS from old to new. These reforms comprise GP fundholders, NHS trusts, and other unfamiliar aspects of an emergent NHS. These chapters look next at the likely impact of reform during the 1990s, and finally at strengths and weaknesses of the new NHS.

The remaining three chapters consider possible health futures. They assess ways forward for the NHS in the three main areas of health care funding, health care delivery and access to health care. In each area they are critical of the present reform programme. However, in suggesting means by which that programme could be improved they do not seek simply to re-create the old NHS.

The NHS is the quintessential element of the British welfare state, purporting to offer universal health coverage on the basis not of income or advantage, but simply of need. Whether it will continue to make this claim at the end of the 1990s is the central question addressed by this book.

1 THE NHS 1948-84

The NHS came into existence on 5 July 1948, the product of a wartime accord agreed by Britain's coalition partners and implemented (with important modifications) by the post-war Labour government. For the first time ever, Britain was provided with a universal health care system.

BRITISH HEALTH CARE PRIOR TO 1948

However, creation of the NHS was by no means the British state's first important initiative in the health sphere. Indeed, the NHS was successor to a series of health care arrangements which, when put together, did in fact amount to quite substantial state-funded provision. The National Insurance Act 1911 had already, for example, extended free care to a number of social groups, such as manual workers and others only receiving up to a certain income. Free drugs and a series of other benefits were also provided by the state by the start of World War One.

The problem with these arrangements – many and varied as they undoubtedly were – was that they were largely ad hoc, comprising no more than a loose patchwork of health care services. Too many people fell through the net of state-funded provision, or found themselves excluded from state schemes on only very modest incomes. More important still was the fact that these uncoordinated arrangements went against the spirit of the post-war times, in lacking a comprehensive, universal and egalitarian character.

TOWARDS A NATIONAL HEALTH SERVICE

Key elements of that spirit were in fact born in the war years themselves. The Attlee Labour government which legislated the NHS into existence built on the Beveridge Report of 1942, which had taken as one of its central assumptions the notion that living standards could only be improved through a comprehensive approach to health care. It was fully supported and underwritten by the wartime coalition government, which in 1943 entered into negotiations with producer groups in health as a means of developing a nationwide system of health care.

Despite a sustained campaign of opposition on the part of the powerful medical profession, chiefly represented by the British Medical Association (BMA), major health reforms were subsequently enacted by the succeeding Attlee government through the National Health Service Act 1946.

The shift from wartime coalition to post-war Labour government did, however, entail changes in state plans for health care provision. In place of Beveridge's decentralised and pluralistic system based on voluntary and municipal (or local authority) hospitals, the Labour Health Secretary, Aneurin Bevan, put a centralised and unitary system based on a nationalised hospital sector. By means of a unified Service he sought to ensure equality of care throughout the country, fearing that decentralisation would undermine such an aspiration. In the light of the present reform programme, which is built around the concept of decentralisation, this was a key change.

FOUNDING PRINCIPLES OF THE NHS

It ensured that the Labour government's plans for the NHS were fully in line with its many other plans, and indeed with the spirit of the age. On the one hand, inspiration behind the NHS was very clearly egalitarian. Access to health care was to be determined not by wealth, privilege or advantage, but by need. On the other, its realisation was conceived in strongly centralist terms. The NHS assumed a classic public sector orientation, being run on the principle of accountability to ministers in parliament.

In truth, however, the NHS was never as pure in conception as was desired by Bevan and his collaborators. From the start it was built on compromise. Opposed to the Labour government and its plans for a comprehensive and unified Service was the medical profession, which was determined not to see its interests wholly undermined by creation of a nationalised health care system. The result of the complicated series of manoeuvres which these two sets of negotiators conducted was an outcome from which both could take substantial satisfaction. The government secured its pledge of a National Health Service. The medical profession ensured that it was not disadvantaged by its creation.

Hospital doctors negotiated an arrangement which allowed them substantial clinical freedom or autonomy provided only that they did not use it to undermine the government's expenditure plans for the NHS. They also retained the right to continue private practice both inside and outside NHS hospitals. General practitioners (GPs) and other primary care providers – dentists, pharmacists and opticians – stayed outside the nationalised Service, being self-employed contractors to the NHS. Community care and health provisions were not brought within the NHS structure at all, but remained a local authority responsibility. Their many protestations notwithstanding, doctors in both hospitals and private practice moved very happily from the ad hoc provisions of years prior to 1948, to the NHS itself. The reason was that the NHS offered them both excellent terms and conditions of employment, and extensive clinical freedom.

The NHS was, then, in no sense unified at the start, and was never to become so. Instead, it assumed a tripartite structure of hospital, GP and community services which was neither unitary nor coherent. Yet the fundamental problem facing the NHS went deeper than this. It was that no sustained – and certainly no successful – attempt had been made to tackle the very great power of the medical profession. The basis of the bargain struck by Bevan and the doctors – in both hospitals and general practice – was that doctors would retain their professional autonomy in return for not placing excessive financial demands on the national exchequer. For many years, both sides stuck to the bargain struck in the post-war years. Ultimately, however, the need to challenge this implicit agreement proved to be an important trigger to Thatcherite reform of the NHS.

The notion that creation of the NHS represented a massive leap in British health care provision is therefore partially undermined both by the extent of previous provision – unsystematic though it certainly often was – and by the compromised character of the NHS itself. Yet the NHS met the demands of post-war Britain. Creation of a tax-funded Service offering universal health care which was free at the point of use was to many a very welcome step in British health care arrangements.

CASH CRISIS

In the short to medium term, the NHS prospered. Indeed, to the extent that it experienced difficulties, they were mainly self-generated. In many ways the NHS was from the start – and continues to be – the victim of its own success. Confounding the expectations of its creators that rapid health improvements would soon cut the cost of health care, the NHS quickly developed the insatiable appetite for resources that has become one of its hallmarks. Costing a mere £444 million, or 3.9 per cent of gross domestic product (GDP), in 1949, its first full year of operation, the NHS has subsequently increased by a factor of four the real level of resources it consumes, and expanded its proportion of GDP to 5.3 per cent. This, it might nevertheless be noted, is a story of extreme parsimony by international standards.

Cash crisis rapidly developed into the single unifying theme which runs through the entire history of the NHS. From its creation, the NHS was 'underfunded', in that demand for health services out-stripped possible supply. Indeed, the first health charges – on spectacles and dentures – were introduced in 1951 by the very Labour administration which had created the NHS in 1948. They provoked the resignation of three ministers, including the architect of the NHS, Nye Bevan, and the future prime minister, Harold Wilson.

The Conservative government which succeeded Labour in October 1951 soon moved to introduce prescription charges. These were charged at one shilling (5p) per form from 1 June 1952. Prescription charges have been a significant feature of the NHS almost ever since. Although they were abolished for three years in the mid 1960s by the Wilson government, and frozen virtually throughout the 1970s, they have since been increased on what is now an annual basis.

It is therefore little surprise that the first commission of inquiry into the NHS was set up, by the Churchill government in 1953, to investigate costs. The Guillebaud Committee, which reported in 1956, absolved the NHS of all charges of wastefulness and inefficiency, arguing instead that the Service was simply under-resourced, its founders having failed to take proper account of the impact on costs of demographic change and inflation. However, the committee did also note that close supervision of the NHS was necessary if costs were not to spiral in future. This line of argument was to be substantially developed in subsequent years.

DRIFT AND INITIATIVE: THE 1950s AND 1960s

The NHS experienced little change in the 1950s, though minor reports on isolated aspects of the Service were produced from time to time. Continuing increases in demand for health care were managed partly by increases in the supply of health services – which grew throughout the decade – and partly by the two mechanisms which were to become central to the NHS's response to increased demand. One was clinical judgment, supposedly exercised solely on the basis of medical assessment of treatment possibilities, but often in fact containing a financial element. The other was waiting lists, which, although they have only become a major aspect of political debate in recent years, have in fact always been an integral part of the Service.

The result of this essentially ad hoc response to increased demand in the 1950s was that the NHS was consigned to drift and loss of direction. Not until Enoch Powell, as Health Minister under Harold Macmillan, produced a Hospital Plan in 1962 was any real or proper thought given to strategic management of it. By this time the NHS was both badly resourced and showing clear evidence that this was the case. Its capital stock was run down, and little attempt had been made to modernise a Service created in the immediate aftermath of war.

Powell's initiative certainly took a strategic view of a central part of the NHS and sought to think seriously through ways in which it could and should develop. However, what was becoming increasingly evident was that the NHS did not really possess mechanisms through which strategic priorities could be developed and implemented. A structural deficiency at the heart of the NHS was becoming apparent. The need to develop strategic capacity through better integration of the NHS emerged as a dominant theme of debate in the 1960s.

It was addressed in largely similar ways by the Labour and Conservative parties. In government until 1970, Labour produced two Green Papers (in July 1968 and February 1970), both of which sought to create a strategic tier of authority within an integrated NHS structure. Initially, area boards were seen as the way forward. Subsequently, regional health authorities were held to be the proper level at which to generate strategy for the NHS. Neither plan was put into operation, because at the general election of June 1970 the Conservatives defeated Labour, and Sir Keith Joseph replaced Richard Crossman at the Department of Health and Social Security (DHSS).

STRUCTURAL REFORM: 1974

The impact on party political debate about NHS reorganisation was, however, marginal. Joseph followed Crossman in placing his faith in a strong regional tier which would act to generate strategic priorities for the NHS. Accordingly, the 1974 reorganisation, enacted on 1 April under the second Wilson administration, but designed by Joseph and his advisers in the previous Conservative government, created 14 Regional Health Authorities (RHAs) in England. These were given responsibility for planning, finance and building, and power to direct the 90 new Area Health Authorities (AHAs) created beneath them. Directly responsible to AHAs were a series of Family Practitioner Committees (FPCs) charged with managing the four branches of primary care (GPs, dentists, pharmacists and opticians). Also integrated into the new structure were community health services, which were transferred from local government to the NHS by the 1974 reforms.

Arrangements in the rest of the UK were rather different because of the strategic capacity already available through the Scottish, Welsh and Northern Ireland Offices. In England, some AHAs were further divided into District Management Teams (DMTs). At the base, Community Health Councils (CHCs) were created to provide a small amount of local accountability in a Service over which full democratic control was only exercised nationally. Their function was, however, only advisory.

Strategic capacity had finally been created through integration of the NHS, and the possibility of a planned NHS had been substantially enhanced. Ironically, Sir Keith Joseph, architect of the strategic system, 'converted' to a new form of Conservatism in the very month that his reforms were enacted, and became, with Margaret Thatcher, the scourge of planning. The impact of this shift in Conservative thinking was to be very great in the 1980s and 1990s. In the 1970s, however, Thatcherite Conservatism was in many ways marginal to mainstream political debate in Britain. The NHS settled into its new planned mode.

The 1974 reorganisation was supplemented in 1976 by development of a new formula for allocating funding within the NHS. Known after the Resource Allocation Working Party which developed it, the RAWP formula established target funding allocations based on a series of variable factors, such as age, sex, and social deprivation. Its immediate impact was to switch funds away from the London region. Its long-term objective was to increase strategic direction of the NHS. By 1976, the NHS was both more integrated and planned than it had ever been, and in possession of a quasi-scientific formula by which resource allocation could be made.

Yet NHS planning was never really successful. On the one hand, each level in the reorganised NHS considered itself capable of making strategic judgments, and none was particularly keen to be dictated to by higher levels. In particular, AHAs – which were explicitly set up to plan resource allocation at the district level – found their plans challenged by DMTs and FPCs. Similar tensions operated between RHAs and AHAs. On the other hand, and far more importantly, no real attempt had been made to address the key independent power centre in the NHS, the medical profession. In consequence, attempts to plan the system according to strategic imperatives developed at regional or area level continued to founder on the rock of professional autonomy. Despite the major restructuring exercise undertaken in the 1970s, the NHS was still largely producer-driven.

HEALTH SERVICE DISCONTENT

The NHS remained a hugely popular institution, but low-level dissatisfaction within its ranks was slowly increasing. In the 1960s it had been GPs who were the chief complainers, feeling that they were losing status in comparison with hospital consultants. A GPs' Charter, implemented in 1966, and increases in GP numbers and payment helped to overcome this source of dissatisfaction. However, far more significant and important sources developed within the hospital sector in the 1970s. Here, first doctors and later other grades of NHS staff were radicalised both by problems with implementation of the structural reform programme of 1974, and by continuing concerns about underfunding. Unionisation increased throughout the decade, particularly among nurses and ancillary grades. In the 1978-79 Winter of Discontent health workers launched their first significant strike.

The response of the Labour government was typical of the times. Challenged on health policy in the mid 1970s, it established a Royal Commission on the NHS in 1976. A large inquiry was launched. However, by the time the Commission reported in July 1979, a new Conservative government had been elected, the Winter of Discontent had altered policy makers' perceptions of the NHS, and political realities had shifted. In truth, the Commission's report included few radical suggestions. It was easily ignored by the incoming Thatcher government.

A similar fate befell a major survey of the health of the nation, *Inequalities in Health*, known (after the chairman of the commission which produced it) as the Black Report. This was submitted to Secretary of State Patrick Jenkin in April 1980. It revealed large differences in health between socio-economic groups, coming to the conclusion that – to put it very crudely – rich people are healthier and live longer than poor. Moreover, the Black Report stated that the NHS had done very little to reduce disparities between different income groups, and had even made matters worse in some respects. Its recommendation was that a broad programme of public action be undertaken, covering not only health services (though these were, of course, seen as central) but also employment, housing and other measures.

The radicalism of the agenda advanced by the Black Report ensured that it was viewed with considerable disfavour by the new government. Very few copies of the report were ever made available by government – though it was subsequently produced in large quantities by others – and these were distributed over the August Bank Holiday week-end of 1980. Jenkin's foreword made it only too clear that the additional £2 billion expenditure called for by the report's authors was unrealistic in any foreseeable circumstances. The Black Report made a major impact on British health debate, but it did little on its own to influence government.

The new Conservative administration was, then, opposed to many of the conclusions of the two major studies which reported in its first year in office. Partly in consequence, Health Service discontent was to remain a dominant feature of Conservative rule in the 1980s and 1990s.

STRUCTURAL REFORM: 1982

The new government had not, however, developed a health policy which was clearly differentiated from that of its predecessors. Little was said about health in the 1979 election manifesto, and the Thatcher administration's first systematic pronouncements, published in December 1979 as *Patients First*, fitted very much into the line of thinking developed during the 1960s and 1970s. Although the title of this first major health paper indicated a commitment to the kind of consumerism which was later to emerge as a central theme of Thatcherite health reforms, its contents revealed no radical initiatives.

Indeed, *Patients First* sought simply (and minimally) to make the existing system work more efficiently and effectively. It explicitly rejected further fundamental reform, and even institution of the kind of line management which was to be pursued with vigour only a few years later. Instead, in the interests of patient care it advocated devolution of control to the lowest possible level, and concomitant improvements in accountability.

The resultant structural reforms of 1982 abolished AHAs, and established a network of 190 District Health Authorities (DHAs) across England. They also instituted a review system which, in the event, turned out to be a better pointer to the direction of Thatcherism's NHS reform programme than was the restructuring of health authorities. Finally, the NHS planning system was simplified, through delegation of authority to managers in individual hospitals. Beyond this, little change was made. The major theme of the 1982 reforms was a cautious attempt to build on the reforms of 1974 and make the existing system function better. On the one hand, a measure of decentralisation was instituted. On the other, decentralised management was made a little more accountable to higher tiers.

As it turned out, the 1982 reforms marked the apotheosis of a form of NHS organisation developed on a continuous basis since 1948. In 1984, the paradigm shift to general management was made. This did not in any sense undermine the notion of a unified NHS. Quite the contrary: the shift to general management was necessary to strategic direction of the Service. However, with the appointment of general managers, the consensus model of NHS management, within which integration and planning had been sought, was decisively undermined. At no point after 1982 were government plans for the NHS conceived in terms of the initial deal struck by Bevan and the doctors. From 1991, the very structure of the NHS was changed.

THE OLD NHS

In classic form, the old NHS was run on two main operating principles: consensus management, which was present from the start in the implicit deal concluded by the government and the medical profession when the NHS was created, and strategic planning, which only properly fed through in the 1970s, when structural reform apparently made strategic direction of the system possible. However, the inherent tension between these two principles was never addressed by the old NHS.

At the level of day-to-day working practices, managers in the old NHS sought chiefly to smooth tensions between different groups of professional people rather than attempting to impose management objectives on them. At the level of system organisation, the formal hierarchy established among health authorities in 1974 did not really function properly, because no mechanism existed whereby doctors could be made responsible to non-doctors. Yet the entire principle of strategic planning rested on the possibility of objectives developed at regional or national level being adhered to further down the system. The absence of well-functioning managerial hierarchies strongly undercut this possibility. Only in the 1980s, with the shift to general management, was this basic tension addressed.

The old NHS was, then, an essentially collegiate system run by a series of professional groups. This made it well equipped to deal with an essentially static environment in which little changed, for existing medical practices and arrangements could then simply be handed down from one generation to the next. It was less well equipped to deal with a changing environment in which strategic choices needed to be made, for in the end the old NHS did not have a satisfactory system for implementing any strategic choices that might be taken. Ineffective management was the first major target of Thatcherite reformers.

2 THE INTRODUCTION OF GENERAL MANAGEMENT

Managerial change was the first distinctive policy initiative of Thatcherite reformers. Even so, the drive to managerial reform took time to develop. The 1982 reforms, outlined in *Patients First*, represented no more than incremental adjustment to the old system of consensus management. Only with the introduction of general management in 1984 was a new managerial philosophy applied to the NHS.

EMERGENCE OF A NEW MANAGERIAL PHILOSOPHY

That new philosophy in many ways embodied the very essence of Thatcherism. The notion that professionals should be subject to the same kinds of accountability and control as are found in contemporary business hierarchies is central to modern Conservative doctrine. Not only medicine, but also less elevated professions such as social work and teaching, have at some time in the period since 1979 felt the pressure of reform. The consequences have, however, been variable.

Though always present in Thatcherism, the new managerial philosophy took time to generate reform proposals in different parts of British professional life. In health, it did not develop a substantial reform agenda until 1984, when the drive towards general management was formally instituted. Elements of the new thinking were, however, evident in isolated initiatives taken by the Thatcher government even in its very early years.

Those initiatives were perhaps not informed by any fully developed overall objective, and were often the product of political circumstance rather than a well-formulated plan, but they certainly fitted with the new managerial philosophy which was fully articulated later in the 1980s. The main early reforms comprised:[1]

- Körner initiative: designed to improve information systems in the NHS, this programme (named after the chairperson of its Steering Group) was launched in February 1980
- Efficiency savings: decreed by the Secretary of State, these were set at 0.2 per cent of total budgets in 1981-82, 0.3 per cent 1982-83, and 0.5 per cent in 1983-84

- Annual review process: this system, launched in 1982, was established to bring together on the one hand the Secretary of State and each RHA chairman, and on the other each RHA and each DHA chairman, to monitor and review NHS operations
- Rayner scrutinies: conducted by teams headed by businessman Derek Rayner of Marks and Spencer, these exercises started in the civil service when the Conservatives entered office in 1979, and were extended to the NHS in 1982; they comprised very quick reviews of efficiency in a specified area of the public sector, and made recommendations for action to secure better value for money
- Central control of manpower: from January 1983
- Performance indicators: the initial list of performance indicators (later known as health service indicators) was issued in September 1983, and established comparative measures of performance in some 70 areas of clinical work, finance, manpower, support services and estate management
- Compulsory competitive tendering (CCT): announced in September 1983, CCT forced the NHS (as it was later to force local government) to put certain specified ancillary services out to competitive tender; the service contract might be won by the existing 'in-house' team, but even that team might not be allowed to remain 'in-house', having instead to become an organisation which contracted services to the NHS
- Forced disposal of surplus property: efficient management of the (large) NHS estate became an important government concern

Each of these initiatives, though perhaps of only marginal significance in itself, contributed to a situation in which a paradigm shift in managerial philosophy was surely only a matter of time. That shift was made in the wake of what has become known as the Griffiths Report.

GRIFFITHS' REPORT

The first systematic attack on the managerial style of the old NHS may be traced to October 1983. In this month a 24-page typed letter was sent by four businessmen to Secretary of State Norman Fowler. This letter, commissioned by Fowler in February 1983 – partly in response to growing parliamentary (and other) criticism of NHS management – proved to be one of the most important and influential contributions to health debate in the 1980s.

In it, the four businessmen, headed by Roy Griffiths, deputy managing director of the food retailer J Sainsbury, noted that the NHS's most obvious failing to men with their background and experience was lack of a clear line management hierarchy. 'In short,' they observed (in a sentence which has become justly celebrated), 'if Florence Nightingale were carrying her lamp through the corridors of the NHS today she would almost certainly be searching for the people in charge.'[2] The businessmen's observations and recommendations were accepted in full by the Secretary of State. The pursuit of what they termed 'general management' had begun.

In the wake of Griffiths' report, all RHAs, DHAs and NHS hospitals (at least in England, which was the main focus of reform) were ordered to appoint general managers by the end of 1985. Moreover, at the peak of the NHS structure, two new bodies were created. One was an NHS Supervisory Board (now the NHS Policy Board), chaired by the Secretary of State. The other was an NHS Management Board (now the NHS Management Executive), chaired by the lead manager in the new managerial hierarchy, soon to be known as the NHS Chief Executive. These two new bodies were intended to enhance coordination and drive at the top of the NHS.

Together, new managers throughout the NHS were to assume responsibility for overall direction and strategic management of the British health care service. A line management function developed on clear business principles was thereby introduced to the NHS. General managers were mainly in position by 1986.

THE ATTACK ON PROFESSIONAL AUTONOMY

The attack on professional autonomy, evident in isolated initiatives from the early 1980s, was conducted in earnest after 1984. A large part of this attack was embodied in the introduction of general management. In place of old-style NHS management, in which professional teams of administrators, finance officers, nursing officers and medical officers came together to plan resource allocation in a consensual manner, there developed a more hierarchical mode. Further parts of the attack comprised management budgets for clinicians, by means of which closer control of clinical spending is sought, and extended use of performance (or health service) indicators, which are used to make comparative assessments of clinicians' performance.

However, such changes were clearly not likely to be implemented without meeting resistance from those groups whose autonomy was at stake. This resistance was handled in two main ways. Nurses were confronted in a mainly direct manner, chiefly during the second term of Thatcher government. In a series of long and often acrimonious disputes, they were successfully subjected to the new managerial structures. In the process, the upper echelons of the old nursing hierarchy were virtually abolished.

Hospital doctors posed a far greater challenge, not simply because of their greater professional status, but also because of their more direct control of NHS resources. The average consultant, by the decisions taken during the course of a single year, spends more than £500 000. To manage this very powerful group of professionals, the government allowed consultants to apply for the new managerial positions (though in practice very few did). It also altered the criteria by which distinction awards – which encompass substantial bonus payments – are made to consultants. They now reflect, in part, commitment to managerial priorities.

General managers themselves were appointed on short-term (usually three-year) rolling contracts, placed on performance-related pay schemes, and subjected to performance review. Outside the ranks of NHS employees, control of GPs was instituted by means of restrictions on drug prescriptions, and similar measures. More developed attacks on nurses and GPs were to follow in later years, with imposition of a regrading exercise on nurses in 1987, and of a new contract on GPs in 1990.

THE NURSES' REGRADING EXERCISE

The nurses' regrading exercise sought to replace an 'unfair' system, in which pay often failed accurately to reflect true levels of responsibility, with one which was 'fairer', in that the link between responsibility and pay was made explicit in a new set of grading criteria. It was not, however, seen in this light by a sizeable proportion of nurses, some of whom (usually at lower grades) incurred financial losses under the new system. The entire exercise provoked substantial discontent among the nursing profession.

Tens of thousands of formal appeals were launched against the regradings published in 1987. Many thousands had still to be heard in the summer of 1992. On the current rate of progress it will take more than a century for the backlog of appeals to be cleared. Some nursing staff have, however, done very well out of the regrading exercise.

Its key achievement was to generate a system of nursing grades which provided management – for the first time ever – with comprehensive information about nursing tasks and abilities. As such, the regrading exercise has produced a system which is essential to efficient management of nursing staff.

THE NEW GPs' CONTRACT

The new GPs' contract stems directly from the 1987 White Paper, *Promoting Better Health*, in seeking both to increase central control of GPs and to improve patient choice and service. It embodies commitments to higher standards of primary care, and to better coverage of vulnerable members of society. In line with this latter commitment, it places increased emphasis on prevention, and gives GPs more incentive to treat poor and disadvantaged sections of the population. Preventive measures – such as screening targets, health promotion clinics, and regular examinations for patients, particularly those 'at risk' – and reformed incentive structures feature strongly in the new arrangements.

Control is extended by means of indicative prescribing amounts, medical audit, and closer monitoring of GPs. Indicative amounts attempt to exert downward pressure on the cost of prescriptions by drawing cost considerations to the attention both of GPs and of health authorities which manage them. This measure is particularly important because of the substantial cost involved. More than a third of the cost of primary care is spent on drugs, which consume more resources than do the salaries of the doctors who prescribe them. Medical audit in the primary sector is a system of peer review of general practice, and is similar to that which has been instituted among hospital consultants.

Choice is furthered by open registration and development of public information. By the new contract individuals have much greater freedom to register with the GP of their choice. To inform this choice, GPs are required to publish a leaflet describing the services they offer. This must include personal details about such matters as age and medical interests. Enhancement of patient service is sought through clear specification of minimum standards. All doctors must be available to see patients for 26 hours a week, spread over five days. They must accept 24-hour responsibility for patients, and to this end are expected to live within a reasonable distance of their practice. In some senses, these latter measures represent little more than a formalisation of existing procedures.

Like the nurses' regrading exercise, development – and eventually imposition – of the new GPs' contract met with a storm of professional protest. Much of this focused on an alleged lack of resources to cover the cost of extra work GPs and their practice staff were required to do in order to meet screening targets and other aspects of the drive towards preventive medicine. Negotiations between government and the BMA were therefore lengthy, lasting from March 1988 to May 1989. At the end of this period, the terms agreed by the BMA leadership were, however, rejected by its membership. Health Secretary Kenneth Clarke chose to ignore this minor setback, published the new contract (with small amendments) in August 1989, and decreed that it would be implemented from 1 April 1990. Despite the major public campaign directed against Clarke by the BMA, this implementation date was met. It might be noted that the new contract has resulted in significant increases in GPs' incomes.

A new dentists' contract, introduced on 1 October 1990, also sought to shift the emphasis towards preventive action by moving away from a pay-ment system based entirely on piecework to one in which continuing care and capitation fees account for some 20 per cent of dental incomes. It encountered less initial problems but provoked major difficulties in the summer of 1992, when the government discovered that its provisions had resulted in a substantial increase in dentists' incomes. This was largely because dentists had been very successful in signing patients and thus in triggering increased capitation payments. The decision of Health Secretary Virginia Bottomley to cut fees for NHS dental work by 7 per cent from July 1992 provoked dentists to threaten to refuse NHS treatment to many patients. In the longer term, dentists may start to abandon NHS work – as some have in fact already done – because of their dislike of the new contractual arrangements.

IMPACT OF THE INTRODUCTION OF GENERAL MANAGEMENT

The new managerialism which general management embodied pene-trated different parts of the NHS to different extents. Ancillary staff were quickly subjected to the new hierarchies, the introduction of

CCT greatly facilitating this process. Nursing staff succeeded in gaining representation in the new management structures, but nevertheless had to concede the principle of professional self-government. Consultants and GPs proved to be a lot more troublesome.

Only very occasionally, however, did they need to indulge in active, public resistance to defend their professional modes of working. This was because the old NHS itself continued to provide them with defence mechanisms. In the absence of developed sources of information – relating to prices and costings in particular – it was very difficult to impose new disciplines on doctors. In many cases they simply worked as in the days before introduction of general management, aware that few possibilities to discipline them existed. However, the real problem was not that information systems remained crude – though certainly they did – but that no real sanction could be brought to bear on consultants' work patterns and behaviour. Clinical autonomy was protected by this lack of a disciplining agent.

The analogy government started to draw was with a competitive market. In the old NHS, no hospital or general practice could be forced to improve its performance by pressure of bankruptcy or even looming losses. In consequence, the degree of control that could be exercised over the key professional group of doctors would always be limited. What was needed was the kind of disciplining agent which faced people in the private sector. Only by this means could clinical autonomy be overcome, and genuine efficiency be secured in the NHS.

REINFORCEMENT OF THE NEW MANAGERIALISM

The internal market reforms of 1991 were therefore designed, in part, to reinforce the new managerialism. In making the purchaser-provider distinction which lies at the heart of these reforms, the landmark White Paper, *Working for Patients*, substantially increased the pressure to replace consensus management with businesslike hierarchies.

It did this by generating something very close to profit and loss criteria within individual NHS units, such as hospitals and general practices. These criteria are not actual measures of profit, for no unit within the NHS is allowed to extract profit from it. They could however turn out to be real measures of loss, for units which fail to pay their way will (it is said) be allowed to disappear from the British health care system. The relevance of this to the new managerialism is that it places a very important sanction on medical behaviour, and substantially reinforces the need for a hierarchical system of management which can direct NHS units according to pressing financial demands.

On top of this extremely important alteration to NHS internal operations, *Working for Patients* also introduced a number of discrete changes to NHS management. In particular, it altered the criteria by which members of health authorities are appointed, cutting back the role of representative groups, and extending the role of genuinely managerial figures. On 26 July 1990 smaller and more streamlined RHAs were created. On 17 September 1990 similar alterations were made to DHAs. Also on this date, FPCs were transformed into Family Health Service Authorities (FHSAs) and given a stronger managerial hold over the primary care sector.

The main impact of *Working for Patients* was, however, contained in its internal market reforms. These embody a very different dynamic from the managerial and regulatory drive of the 1980s. They are analysed in detail in Chapter 5.

CULTURAL CHANGE IN THE NHS

Thatcherism spent most of the 1980s trying to make the old NHS work better than had hitherto been the case. The means to this end, it decided, was managerial reform. Another restructuring exercise was explicitly rejected by Griffiths, who sought rapid alteration to the existing NHS rather a more lengthy process of extended debate followed by major structural reform.

The result was certainly substantial cultural change. Even before the internal market reforms were introduced there were clear signs that the new managerialism was altering the way in which the NHS functioned. Ancillary staff had been brought entirely within its remit. Nursing grades were largely subject to the new managerial hierarchies. Doctors, however, retained substantial clinical autonomy. This was only really threatened by the internal market reforms of 1991.

The NHS at the end of the 1980s was therefore in the throes of managerial change. Its culture was clearly altering in line with the paradigm shift to general management, but it had not yet been entirely transformed. In the process, a great deal of resistance and continuing discontent had been generated. This was partly because the move to general management was associated by many with alleged cuts in NHS funding – the recurrent theme of the 1980s – and partly because it did in fact represent a clear attack on existing working practices.

The NHS which entered the 1990s was certainly more businesslike than had been the case previously. It possessed a dynamism and sense of managerial initiative that were unprecedented. Nevertheless, its underlying principles remained unchallenged. Until the start of the 1990s, the NHS continued to aspire to – though it did not actually deliver – unity, and equality of treatment throughout the UK. Indeed, institution of a managerial hierarchy actually increased capacity for strategic direction of the NHS.

The reforms which were to undermine these principles, and alter the essential character of the NHS (from old to new) did not emerge until 1989, and were not implemented until 1991. This second major element of Thatcherism's reform of the NHS involved deliberate fragmentation of the system, and is currently taking place. Far more radical than the pursuit of general management, it is analysed in later chapters. First, however, the facts and figures of the NHS's contentious experience of Thatcherism, and its standing in an international context, are assessed.

NOTES

1. For a full discussion, see S Harrison, *Managing the National Health Service: Shifting the Frontier?* (Chapman and Hall, London, 1988).
2. R Griffiths, *NHS Management Inquiry* (DHSS, London, 1983), p.12.

3 FACTS AND FIGURES OF THE THATCHER DECADE

The NHS was subjected to a managerial revolution in the 1980s, and even found its basic character challenged by the occasional ideological foray from New Right individuals and think tanks. However, until the internal market reforms of 1991 began to be implemented, the fundamental principles on which it rests were almost entirely untouched by radical reform. It may seem an odd description of a very turbulent decade, but the 1980s were in some ways rather stable years for the NHS. Stability is indeed a central impression to emerge from analysis of facts and figures of the Thatcher decade.

UNDERFUNDING

The vexed issue of funding was undoubtedly the focus of debate throughout the Thatcher years, with the figure of £2 billion underfunding being regularly quoted by the end of those years. It was derived from extrapolations of health spending in the 1970s, when real annual increases of around 2 per cent were recorded.

Yet the statistics of the Thatcher years seem to tell a rather different story. The bare figures reproduced in Table 3.1 (overleaf) show that the amount of money spent on the NHS rose throughout the period 1979-90, and that it has continued to do so. This is the case without exception, and is not simply a product of inflation. It holds true in real terms. NHS spending throughout the UK has risen in actual terms from £7.8 billion in 1978-79, the last year of Labour government, to a planned £34.4 billion in the current year, 1992-93. In real terms (1990-91 prices) it has risen from £19.9 billion to £30.8 billion over the same period.

This is a real increase of 55 per cent, and takes the proportion of public spending claimed by health from precisely 12 per cent in 1978-79 to almost certainly more than 14 per cent in 1992-93. The Health Department (which funds only the English part of the NHS) overtook Defence in 1990-91 to become the second biggest spender in the public sector, behind Social Security.

Table 3.1: UK health spending, 1978-79 to 1994-95

	Expenditure on health £ bn	Real expenditure on health £ bn (1990-91)	Health as % total public expenditure
1978-79	7.8	19.9	12.0
1979-80	9.3	20.3	12.1
1980-81	12.0	22.0	13.0
1981-82	13.5	22.6	13.0
1982-83	14.7	22.9	12.6
1983-84	15.5	23.2	12.7
1984-85	16.7	23.7	12.7
1985-86	17.6	23.8	12.7
1986-87	18.9	24.7	12.9
1987-88	20.7	25.6	13.4
1988-89	22.8	26.4	14.1
1989-90	24.7	26.8	13.8
1990-91	27.7	27.7	14.2
1991-92 (est)	31.4	29.4	14.4
1992-93 (planned)	34.4	30.8	n/a
1993-94 (planned)	36.6	31.5	n/a
1994-95 (planned)	38.5	32.2	n/a

Note: Department of Health spending is often quoted as total NHS spending. In the current year, 1992-93, the figure is £27.4 billion. However, this statistic only covers health spending in England. It does not include health spending in Scotland, Wales and Northern Ireland, which feeds through their respective territorial Offices. The figures quoted here take account of NHS spending throughout the UK. As can be seen, the planned 1992-93 NHS budget for the UK as a whole is £34.4 billion.
Source: H M Treasury, *Public Expenditure Analyses to 1994-95: Statistical Supplement to the 1991 Autumn Statement*, Cm 1920 (HMSO, London, 1992).

However, to get a true picture of Thatcherism's health spending record, it must be noted that a 55 per cent real increase in NHS funding over 14 years does not mean that the NHS has increased its health care output by this amount. Large amounts of the increased funding have, in fact, been consumed by three factors, each of which makes the NHS inflation rate higher than the standard retail price measure. These three factors are wages (which take more than 70 per cent of NHS resources), technological advance, and an ageing population.

An indication of the impact of the latter factor alone is given by Table 3.2, which shows that on average in 1989-90 the over-85s cost the NHS eighteen times as much as the 5-15 age group, and sixteen times as much as the 16-44 age group.

Table 3.2: Estimated health spending per head, England, 1989-90

Age group	Estimated per capita spending £
Births	1360
0-14	205
5-15	105
16-44	115
45-64	255
65-74	545
75-84	1015
85+	1875

Source: Department of Health, OPCS, H M Treasury, *The Government's Expenditure Plans 1992-93 to 1994-95: Department of Health and Office of Population Censuses and Surveys: Departmental Report*, Cm 1913 (HMSO, London, 1992).

The fact that the inflation rate faced by the NHS is greater than the standard GDP deflator used by government statisticians makes it extremely difficult to determine what actually did happen to NHS funding in the 1980s. This uncertainty itself helped substantially to raise the political temperature in the Thatcher years, as all sides could justifiably pick holes not only in their opponents' arguments, but also in their statistics.

One authoritative study of the real course of NHS funding has, however, been published. It does not cover the full period of Thatcher government, but does at least give an indication of the extent to which increases in funding during the 1980s were sufficient to cover the unique financial pressures faced by the NHS. The result, reproduced in modified form in Table 3.3 (overleaf), is an essentially static picture, in which demand and supply for NHS services kept broadly in step in the 1980s.

Critics of the government might object that the financial requirements of technological change are not fully captured in statistics of this kind, and that they therefore present an unduly favourable record. The government itself could counter that its efficiency drive made a given amount of resources go farther in the 1980s than in previous decades, and that these figures therefore decisively understate the health of the NHS. Indeed, this is precisely the argument that Thatcher in particular sought to develop, insisting on repeated occasions that relevant measures of NHS performance focus not on inputs but on outputs.

Table 3.3: UK health services and needs, 1978-79 to 1986-87

	Volume[1] (1978-79 = 100)	Needs[2] (1978-79 = 100)
1978-79	100	100
1979-80	100	102
1980-81	105	103
1981-82	106	103
1982-83	107	104
1983-84	106	104
1984-85	107	105
1985-86	108	106
1986-87	107	107

1 Volume of UK health care services provided by the NHS using a special NHS deflator taken from the National Income Blue Book.
2 Department of Health index of UK health needs based on the changing demographic structure of the population.
Source: J Le Grand, D Winter and F Woolley, 'The National Health Service: Safe in Whose Hands?', in J Hills (ed), *The State of Welfare: The Welfare State in Britain since 1974* (Clarendon Press, Oxford, 1990), 88-134.

It is certainly the case that NHS efficiency, productivity and outputs increased markedly in the 1980s. In the hospital sector, efficiency gains were substantial. This can be seen from Table 3.4, which registers increases in all aspects of patient treatment.

Table 3.4: Acute hospital services: increases in patient through-put, England, 1974-86

	% increase, 1974-86
Inpatients	21
Day cases	144
Outpatients	14
Accident and emergency	7

Source: DHSS, quoted in B Connah and R Pearson, *NHS Handbook*, 7th ed. (NAHAT/ Macmillan, London, 1991).

A similar picture emerges from Table 3.5, which isolates the various ways in which efficiency in the acute sector was increased, and estimated unit costs were correspondingly reduced.

Table 3.5: Changes in acute hospital services, England, 1974-86

	1974	1986	Change
Average length of stay (days)	10.4	7.6	-2.8
Average turnover interval (days)	3.8	2.5	-1.3
Average throughput (patients per bed)	25.6	36.3	+10.7
Unit costs (estimated £ per patient)	870.0	725.0	-145.0

Note: Turnover interval = number of days a bed is unoccupied between patients; throughput = discharges and deaths per available bed.
Source: Ibid.

Faced with statistical conflict of this kind, it must simply be admitted that no perfect measure of health care outcomes will ever be produced, and that the best course in this situation is to stick to the notion of real funding stability which emerges from authoritative accounts. The NHS probably did not suffer financially during the Thatcher years. It probably did not prosper either.

SOURCES OF FUNDING

Within the overall NHS funding regime, a highly contentious issue in the Thatcher decade was the increasing diversity of funding sources. On the one hand, hospitals in particular were encouraged to make more efficient use of the resources which they control, either through land sales or through shopping malls and other fundraising ventures. On the other, charges embarked on a long upward trend in 1979.

Indeed, prescription charges have risen dramatically during the period of Conservative government. In 1979 they stood at 20p per item. By 1992 they had been increased to £3.75, a rise of nearly 1800 per cent in actual terms, and of nearly 600 per cent in real terms. The contribution of prescription charges to NHS funding has not, however, increased to the same extent.

This is for two main reasons. First, at the same time as prescription charges have been increased, so too has the range of exemptions from charges been extended. Indeed, an odd aspect of ritual denunciation of prescription charge increases in the 1980s was repeated reference to the plight of poor, aged and needy people who do not, in fact, pay for prescriptions. The second main reason is that categories of the population which are exempt from charges are also principal consumers of drugs. Whilst the annual number of items prescribed to persons aged 64 or below averages five, for the 65-74 age group it averages 12, and for those aged over 75 it averages 24. Indeed, 96 per cent of all prescription growth between 1977 and 1988 was accounted for by medicines for the elderly, with the result that in 1990 more than 41 per cent of all NHS prescriptions were written for people of state pension age. The vast majority of all prescriptions are now free.[1]

Table 3.6: NHS funding sources, England, 1978-79 to 1991-92

	Total public expenditure[1] %	Charges %	Other[2] %
1978-79	97.5	2.2	0.3
1979-80	97.4	2.3	0.3
1980-81	97.2	2.5	0.3
1981-82	97.0	2.7	0.3
1982-83	96.9	2.8	0.3
1983-84	96.6	3.0	0.4
1984-85	96.5	3.0	0.5
1985-86	96.4	2.9	0.7
1986-87	95.8	3.1	1.1
1987-88	95.7	2.9	1.4
1988-89	95.2	3.1	1.7
1989-90	94.1	4.5	1.4
1990-91 (est)	94.1	4.2	1.7
1991-92 (est)	94.3	4.0	1.7

1 Sources are general taxation and the NHS element in national insurance contributions.
2 Mainly capital receipts from land sales.
Source: Department of Health, OPCS, H M Treasury, op cit.

The consequence is that very little change to NHS core funding has yet been made. As can be seen from Table 3.6, taxation remains the main source. Although the contribution of charges and other funding sources to NHS finance has risen throughout the period since 1979, it remains extremely marginal.

WAITING LISTS

Linked to debate in the 1980s of funding was public concern about the length of NHS waiting lists. These were popularly held to be a clear indication of NHS underfunding, and of the misguided nature of health policy. Waiting lists were certainly long in the 1980s, but again the issue is less straightforward than it might seem to be.

The first reason for this is that waiting lists, far from being a reliable and objective measure of changes in government policy, are in fact both unreliable and in many ways subjective. They are unreliable for a number of reasons, among which are changing definitions of 'waiting', and the fact that people tend to remain on waiting lists even if they have moved house, discovered that they no longer need the operation in question, or died. They are subjective because they are constructed not by a disinterested party, but by the very people who subsequently use them to campaign for greater NHS resources. It is doctors who control entry to waiting lists, and they who employ them in campaigns for increased NHS funding. This second difficulty is probably more substantial than the first.[2]

Waiting lists are, then, a decidedly unscientific measure of NHS resource gaps. Their other striking aspect is that they are by no means a new or recent feature of the NHS. In fact, waiting lists have always been a tool of health care rationing in the UK. However, they only began to feature at the very centre of health debate when the NHS was strongly politicised at the end of the 1970s. Indeed, the first College of Health *Guide to Hospital Waiting Lists* was not published until 1984, even though the DHSS had been collecting data for some time before that.

Table 3.7: Hospital waiting lists for England at 31 March, 1979-92[1]

Year	Thousands	Year	Thousands
1979	752.4	1986	673.1
1980	664.9	1987	687.9
1981	628.3	1988	876.3
1982	622.5	1989	922.7
1983	726.2	1990	958.9
1984	692.9	1991	948.2
1985	674.5	1992	915.0[2]

1 Inpatient and day cases combined, including self-deferrals.
2 Provisional.
Source: Department of Health.

The statistics reproduced in Table 3.7 show that popular belief is right to hold that waiting lists were high in the 1980s, but wrong to hold that they were consistently high by the standards of the late 1970s at least. Indeed, throughout the 1970s waiting lists for NHS treatment in England were around 750 000. Previously, in the quarter-century after creation of the Service in 1948, they had stood at around 500 000. They dipped slightly in the early and mid 1980s, only exceeding the March 1979 total for England as late as 1988. Thereafter the situation clearly did deteriorate substantially.

Similarly, the highly sensitive total of people who have been on a waiting list for more than one year remained remarkably stable throughout the Thatcher years, usually standing very close to – or at – the 25 per cent registered in 1979. In 1991, for the first time, this figure was brought down to 20 per cent. Further targeted spending by the Department of Health – in line with *Patient's Charter* commitments – reduced it to around 15 per cent by the time of the 1992 general election.

NHS EMPLOYMENT

As might be expected from the impression of stability created by the above statistics, total NHS employment in the UK remained broadly stable during the 1980s at around one million (thereby confirming the NHS as the biggest employer in Europe). The figures quoted in Table 3.8 show a 3 per cent fall in numbers employed in the NHS between 1981 and 1990. This is a very small change in 10 years.

Table 3.8: NHS employment, UK, 1981-90

	1981 '000	1990 '000	Percentage change 1981-90	Staff group as % of of total staff (1990)
Medical and dental	49.7	56.1	+ 12.9	5.6
Nursing/midwifery	492.8	505.2	+ 2.5	50.5
Professional/technical	80.2	103.0	+ 28.4	10.3
Administrative/clerical	133.3	159.2	+ 19.4	15.9
Ancillary	220.1	127.6	– 42.0	12.8
Other non-medical	56.2	48.4	– 13.9	4.8
Total	1032.2	999.5	– 3.2	100.0

Note: Figures are whole-time equivalents.
Source: Central Statistical Office, *Social Trends 22* (HMSO, London, 1992).

The global total does, however, obscure two important changes which partially offset each other. One is the fall in numbers of ancillary staff (occasioned chiefly by contracting out legislation). The other is the rise in qualified staff. Since work previously undertaken by directly-employed ancillary staff is now undertaken by contracted staff, there was probably a real rise in NHS employment in the 1980s, though again the total change can only have been small in percentage terms. The rise in numbers of professionals is claimed as a major achievement by government ministers.

It should also be noted that the total number of family practitioners – doctors, dentists, pharmacists and opticians – rose in the 1980s. These people are not directly employed by the NHS, but are instead self-employed contractors for NHS business. Their numbers do not therefore appear in NHS employment statistics. To cite figures relating only to GPs, BMA statistics show an increase in total numbers in Britain from 25 614 in 1979 to 30 631 in 1989. The trend increase in fact stretches back to the late 1960s. Numbers of practice staff have also risen markedly in recent years. Similarly, in the other three branches of primary care, total numbers rose continuously throughout the 1980s. The single exception is contracting pharmacists, who registered a slight fall in numbers in 1988-89.

THE PRIVATE SECTOR

A final index of NHS experience of the 1980s may perhaps be found in health insurance registrations, for these are likely to rise, at least partially, in response to concern about, and dissatisfaction with, state-funded health care services.

Here, the data show a dramatic increase since 1979. Indeed, during the course of the 1980s a significant number of people expressed dissatisfaction with the NHS by voting with their feet – or, rather, their cheque books and credit cards – and buying private health care, either directly or through an insurance scheme provided by the likes of BUPA, Private Patients Plan and Western Provident Association. By 1988, 5.7 million Britons, or some 10 per cent of the population, had some form of private health insurance, though often it was not comprehensive. This was twice as many as in 1979. BUPA was the dominant health insurer, holding a market share in 1988 of 60 per cent.[3]

Other measures confirm the switch to private health care in the 1980s. It is of course the case that estimates of the extent of independent health care depend very much on measures used. Possible candidates for inclusion range from the most obvious category of elective surgery in independent hospitals, to the many varieties of primary care which are provided outside the NHS, to long-term care in residential homes and the like, to, finally, the increasingly important sector of alternative medicine. In these circumstances, no precise measure of change in the purchase of health care from the independent sector can be given. However, a standard source, the *NHS Handbook*, quotes statistics which show that the proportion of UK hospital-based treatment and care provided by the independent sector increased from 7.5 per cent in 1984 to 15.3 per cent in 1989.

It is highly probable that recession since the late 1980s has severely affected the independent health sector. However, the extent of private provision is still likely to be substantially greater in the 1990s than it was in the 1970s, as indeed is only to be expected after a decade in which marginal changes in tax policy have increased the inducement to go private, particularly among older people (who consume most NHS resources). Whilst the government's target private insurance coverage of 25 per cent by 1990 came nowhere near being met, there has clearly been a significant move in this direction.

In part this can be put down to dissatisfaction with the NHS, in part to changes in government policy and to a surge in affluence, especially for the better-off, in the middle part of the 1980s. However, a cultural shift must also account for some of the change. The biggest increase in private insurance came as early as 1980, and resulted largely from companies adding health cover to the remuneration package they were prepared to offer top executives.

Indeed, it may be that cultural factors were the most important determinants of increased health insurance in the 1980s, for evidence of a cultural shift may be found in many other aspects of contemporary health debate. The most telling perhaps relates to the contentious issue of waiting lists. As has already been noted, these have always been a feature of the NHS. Only in the 1980s, however, did the British public come to view them as negative comment on the nation's health care system, and demand action to reduce them. Previous passivity with regard to the NHS had been transformed into a much more active and militant stance.

STABILITY AND CHANGE IN THE THATCHER DECADE

Facts and figures of the Thatcher decade present a picture of remarkable stability. NHS funding, service and employment levels remained largely static throughout the 1980s. Yet the final index of NHS experience of the 1980s cited here – that which relates to the private sector – demonstrates that stability could not remain the watchword of the NHS for very much longer. Increased health insurance registrations indicate that the NHS faced a growing challenge in the 1980s, prompted either by extensive dissatisfaction with the service it provided, or by an important cultural shift towards increased choice in health care arrangements.

In the 1980s, this growing challenge formed the context in which general management, with its strong emphasis on efficiency, was developed. In the 1990s, it would be met by the internal market reforms, which seek to promote both efficiency and responsiveness in the NHS.

Indications of NHS stability in the Thatcher decade are therefore only partially reliable. They accurately reflect respect throughout the 1980s for the underlying principles on which the NHS was founded. They fail, however, to reveal the very great policy challenges with which it was increasingly confronted.

NOTES

1. D Taylor and A Maynard, *Medicines, the NHS and Europe: Balancing the Public's Interests* (King's Fund Institute and Centre for Health Economics, London and York, 1990).
2. On these two difficulties, see P Day and R Klein, 'Britain's Health Care Experiment', *Health Affairs* 10,3 (Fall 1991), 39-59.
3. For a more extensive discussion of the rise of private health insurance in the 1980s, see N Johnson, *Reconstructing the Welfare State: A Decade of Change 1980-1990* (Harvester Wheatsheaf, Hemel Hempstead, 1990), ch.4.

4 THE NHS IN INTERNATIONAL CONTEXT

In the 1980s the NHS faced a number of new policy challenges. Some were the product of Thatcherism's ideological drive. Others, however, derived from changed socio-economic circumstances and broad cultural shifts. The NHS was thereby forced to deal with issues which were also confronting other health systems. Indeed, throughout the world the 1980s and 1990s have witnessed health care systems in transition.

INTERNATIONAL HEALTH CARE SYSTEMS

Health care systems vary across the world. However, in contemporary industrialised societies they usually conform to one of four basic types, each of which mixes public and private sector roles in a different way.

At the extremes of possible provision are a fully nationalised health service, and a fully privatised one. In between them are systems of health insurance organised either directly by the state, or indirectly through compulsory individual health insurance programmes (known as social insurance). No health care system conforms exactly to either of the extreme positions, though the British comes closest to full nationalisation, and the American comes closest to full privatisation. Even these systems deviate markedly from the extremes.

On the one hand, the British NHS coexists with a reasonably substantial private health care sector. On the other, and far more strikingly, the American voluntary system coexists with federal and state programmes which manage to consume almost as large a proportion of GDP as does the NHS without coming close to providing a comprehensive service. Of the intermediate positions, the state insurance position is best represented by Canada and Australia, whilst social insurance systems are to be found in many European states, notably France, Germany and Holland.

COST

A key challenge faced by all health care systems is rising costs. That challenge is better managed in the UK than in many other countires. All international comparisons demonstrate that the most striking aspect of the NHS is the small amount of resources it consumes. A recent study of 24 OECD countries confirms that the UK gets its health care system very much on the cheap. It is reproduced in Table 4.1.

Table 4.1: Health care expenditures in 24 OECD countries, 1989

	Percent of GDP	Per capita health spending[1]	As % UK spend	% public spending
Turkey	3.9	175	2	37
Greece	5.1	371	44	89
United Kingdom	5.8	836	100	87
Portugal	6.3	464	56	62
Spain	6.3	644	77	78
Denmark	6.3	912	109	84
Japan	6.7	1035	124	73
New Zealand	7.1	820	98	85
Finland	7.1	1067	128	79
Belgium	7.2	980	117	89
Ireland	7.3	658	79	84
Luxembourg	7.4	1193	143	92
Italy	7.6	1050	126	79
Australia	7.6	1125	135	70
Norway	7.6	1234	148	95
Switzerland	7.8	1376	165	68
Austria	8.2	1093	131	67
Germany	8.2	1232	147	72
Netherlands	8.3	1135	136	73
Iceland	8.6	1353	162	88
France	8.7	1274	152	75
Canada	8.7	1683	201	75
Sweden	8.8	1361	163	90
United States	11.8	2354	282	42
Average	**7.4**	**1059**	–	**76**

1 In US dollars, GDP purchasing power parities.
Source: Adapted from G J Schieber, J-P Poullier and L M Greenwald, 'Health Care Systems in Twenty-Four Countries', *Health Affairs* 10,3 (Fall 1991), 22-38.

One consequence of the NHS's comparative parsimony is that the issue of underfunding which has dominated recent health debate in Britain has as its counterpart in most other health systems the issue of overfunding, or cost explosion. This is particularly true of the United

States, which has in every respect an extraordinary health care spending record. At almost 12 per cent of GDP – indeed, it is said now to be more than 12 per cent – and at $2354 per capita (in 1989 prices), the US dramatically out-spends every country in the health sphere. It might be noted here that, if the anomalous case of Turkey is disregarded, the US figure of only 42 per cent public spending is also a distant outlier.

It might therefore seem that in the sphere of funding the NHS faces very different challenges from most – if not all – other health care systems. In a sense, it does. However, both underfunding in Britain and overfunding almost everywhere else have one common feature. This is the tension between growing demands for health care and increasing costs of supply. In Britain, demand has been limited and charges of underfunding have resulted. Elsewhere, health care provision has been expanded at the cost of spiralling spending. The structural problem is similar in each case.

EFFECTIVENESS

Despite the limited amount of resources spent on health care in the UK, the service provided by the NHS performs well by standard measures of effectiveness. These measures are to be treated with some caution, partly because it is not clear how exactly effectiveness is to be assessed – the measures used here areinfant and perinatal mortality, and life expectancy – and partly because many other factors besides a national health care system contribute to health outcomes. Nevertheless, there must be some value in the finding that Britons do not seem to be adversely affected by the low cost of the NHS.

A simple comparison of UK health outcome statistics with those of the same 24 OECD countries already used for cost comparison indicates that UK figures are at the very least good, and often better than that. Table 4.2 (overleaf) reproduces these figures.

Where the UK does slip below the OECD average – in perinatal mortality, and female life expectancy at birth – it is only by a very marginal amount. In passing, it might be noted that the United States, for all its massive spending on health care, registers mainly average health outcomes.

Table 4.2: Health outcome measures in 24 OECD countries, 1988

	Infant mortality live births per 1000	Perinatal mortality deaths per 1000	Male life expectancy at birth (yrs)	Female life expectancy at birth (yrs)
Australia	8.7	10.7	73.1	79.5
Austria	8.1	7.4	72.0	78.6
Belgium	9.4	10.4	71.4	78.2
Canada	7.2	7.6	73.0	79.7
Denmark	7.5	8.7	71.8	77.7
Finland	6.1	6.5	70.7	78.7
France	7.7	9.2	72.3	80.6
Germany	7.6	6.5	71.8	78.4
Greece	11.0	12.9	74.1	78.9
Iceland	6.2	7.5	74.6	79.7
Ireland	8.6	10.4	71.0	76.7
Italy	9.3	12.3	72.7	79.4
Japan	4.8	6.2	75.5	81.3
Luxembourg	9.4	7.1	70.6	77.9
Netherlands	6.8	9.2	73.3	79.9
New Zealand	10.8	8.5	71.0	77.3
Norway	8.3	7.9	73.1	79.6
Portugal	13.0	15.3	70.7	77.6
Spain	8.1	10.6	73.2	79.8
Sweden	5.8	6.8	74.2	80.0
Switzerland	6.8	7.6	73.9	80.7
Turkey	65.0	–	63.2	68.1
United Kingdom	9.0	9.1	72.4	78.1
United States	10.0	9.7	71.5	78.3
Average	**10.6**	**9.0**	**72.1**	**78.5**

Note: In a few cases, data relate to slightly earlier years than 1988.
Source: Ibid.

POPULARITY

Like effectiveness, popularity is difficult to measure. However, data exist by means of which it is possible to gain at least an indication of comparative popularity ratings.

Table 4.3: Health care satisfaction in 10 OECD countries, 1990

	Minor change needed	Fundamental change needed	Rebuild system completely
Canada	56	38	5
Netherlands	47	46	5
France	41	42	10
Germany	41	35	13
Australia	34	43	17
Sweden	32	58	6
Japan	29	47	6
United Kingdom	27	52	17
Italy	12	46	40
United States	10	60	29

Source: R Amara, 'Health Care: Some International Comparisons', in Blue Cross of California and The King's Fund, *Health Care in the '90s: A Global View of Delivery and Financing* (BCC and KFI, California, 1991), 7-18.

In a small study of 10 OECD nations conducted in 1990, and reproduced in Table 4.3, the NHS for the first time fares badly in international comparison. Only Italy and the United States register a lower approval rating. At first sight, this is an unexpected result. It conflicts not only with anecdotal evidence, but also with opinion surveys which regularly demonstrate strong support for the NHS.

The key to resolving this apparent inconsistency lies in distinguishing between the principle of a National Health Service, and recent experience of its functioning. Whilst the British public remains strongly committed to the idea of state-sponsored health care – the figure registered by *British Social Attitudes* in both 1985 and 1990 was 98 per cent support – it has become increasingly dissatisfied with the current state of the NHS. This too has been registered by *British Social Attitudes*, which shows overall dissatisfaction levels rising from 26 per cent in 1983 to 47 per cent in 1990 (they were probably even higher in intervening years, notably 1987). At the top of all lists of required NHS improvements have for many years been hospital waiting lists for non-emergency operations.

The central problem with the NHS would seem to be the lack of choice and responsiveness which are inherent in it. In a survey series conducted in the 1960s and 1970s by the right-wing Institute of Economic Affairs (IEA) this problem emerges both clearly and increasingly. This series is reproduced in Table 4.4 (overleaf).

Table 4.4: Policy for health, Great Britain, 1963-78

	1963 %	1965 %	1970 %	1978 %
Keep present system	41	32	29	20
Concentrate on poor	24	25	24	18
Allow contracting out	33	34	46	54
Don't know	2	9	1	7

Source: R Harris and A Seldon, *Over-Ruled on Welfare: The Increasing Desire for Choice in Education and Medicine and Its Frustration by 'Representative' Government* (IEA, London, 1979).

It may be that perceived government hostility to the NHS has altered policy preferences for health in years since 1979. These are nevertheless striking figures.

GLOBAL HEALTH CARE REFORM

International comparison demonstrates that the configuration of pressures facing the NHS in the 1980s was unusual. Most health care systems were both more expensive and more responsive than was the NHS. Yet whether the starting point is the NHS or a health care system in another industrialised country, the target finishing point is the same. The search for a health care system which is both cheap and responsive is being conducted across the world.

This search is generating remarkable convergence in health care reform programmes. A 1991 survey of seven European nations – Belgium, France, Germany, Holland, Ireland, Spain and the UK – demonstrates that all are coming to rely on what may be called the 'public contract' model of health care.[1] In this model, health care is funded globally but delivered in a decentralised manner through some form of market system. It thereby combines cost containment with choice, precisely the attributes which are currently sought by health care reformers the world over.

In consequence, common strategies are being pursued within the global health reform movement. On the funding side, attempts to place overall limits on costs – and particularly on open-ended funding arrangements – are highly visible. On the delivery side, the issue of health care pluralism in a market for care is a central theme. It is producing moves towards both increased competition and increased regulation of individuals and institutions in the care market.

Caught in the reformist drive is medical autonomy. Whether the primary motivation is to control costs or to increase choice and responsiveness, governments are seeking to undermine a crucial power bloc within national health care systems. In the case of the UK, early aspects of this attempt have already been reviewed in the general management reforms. Later aspects, embodied in the internal market programme, are reviewed in subsequent chapters. Reform along both lines is evident in many other health care systems.

NHS reform is, then, by no means a unique or even unusual phenomenon. Throughout the world demand and supply side pressures are combining to force governments to enact health care reforms which reflect the public contract model. All that is unusual about Britain is the point of departure for health care reform: an inexpensive and unresponsive health care system.

NOTE

1. J W Hurst, 'Reforming Health Care in Seven European Nations', *Health Affairs* 10,3 (Fall 1991), 7-21.

5 THE INTERNAL MARKET REFORMS

Radical reform of the NHS came not with the introduction of general management in 1984, but with the shift to an internal market for NHS business in 1991. Since then, the old unitary – if never really unified – NHS has been increasingly fragmented. Its basic character is in the process of fundamental alteration.

THE DECISION TO EMBARK ON MAJOR REFORM

Like many other policy initiatives – not only in health – the internal market reform programme was the product of many factors. No hint of fundamental reform of the NHS was included in the Conservatives' 1987 manifesto, and it is generally believed that the administration intended to postpone radical health measures to its fourth term (then confidently and, as it turned out, correctly awaited). Yet in January 1988 – little more than six months after the 1987 election – an NHS Review was announced by Margaret Thatcher, and exactly a year later the conclusions reached by the review team were published in the key White Paper, *Working for Patients*.

The factors which combined to generate the 1988 NHS Review and the resultant report, *Working for Patients*, were a mix of pressing political circumstance and firmly-held political conviction. Political circumstances became pressing for the Thatcher administration almost immediately after it had secured its third successive election victory in June 1987. Not for the first time in the 1980s, the NHS entered a period in which alleged underfunding became a leading news item.

Indeed, the British media in the late autumn of 1987 was dominated by accounts of ward closures, and by expressions of unease on the part of the medical profession. Financial problems in the NHS appeared to be more acute than ever. This impression was reinforced in December 1987 when the presidents of three Royal Colleges publicly voiced concerns about the financial health of the NHS. It was given a very sharp focus when children with cardiac problems were forced to join long waiting lists because of financial difficulties at Birmingham Children's Hospital. £101 million was immediately injected into the NHS.

It was clear, however, that this would not be enough to overcome the Conservatives' problems. Faced with mounting difficulties, Margaret Thatcher decided to abandon the essentially low profile she had long adopted with regard to the NHS – summed up in her defensive statement of 1982, that the NHS was 'safe' in Conservative hands – and to take the political initiative. In the course of an interview on the BBC current affairs programme, *Panorama*, on 25 January 1988, she announced to an unsuspecting nation (and, it is thought, Cabinet) that an NHS Review would be established, and that she would chair it. At this point, firmly-held political conviction was applied to the pressing political circumstances of the NHS.

THE DECISION TO ESCHEW REVOLUTIONARY REFORM

Yet in this extremely sensitive policy field there remained clear limits even to Thatcherite political conviction. The review was established to consider the most acute problem facing the NHS, that of funding. However, it quickly eschewed all radical initiative in this sphere, Thatcher firmly proclaiming in her foreword to the resultant White Paper that 'The National Health Service will continue to be available to all, regardless of income, and to be financed mainly out of general taxation'. This commitment was reiterated on the first page of the White Paper's introduction.

It would seem that alternative modes of funding the NHS were considered by the review team, but that each was quickly ruled out on grounds of cost. The British scheme of funding the NHS out of general taxation, which places the Treasury in a strategic position to police annual increases in NHS revenues, is by some distance the cheapest means of financing a comprehensive health care system. This was shown in Chapter 4. Here, Thatcherite radicalism, which is thought to have favoured a shift towards a more individualistic system on something close to American lines, was forced to acknowledge the weight of available evidence, and to take a highly pragmatic stance.

INFLUENCES ON THE NHS REVIEW

Yet radicalism nevertheless exercised a clear influence on the review team, and is very much in evidence in its report. If *Working for Patients* takes a conservative line on NHS funding, it takes a radical line on NHS organisation and management. In this area, the review team was besieged with suggestions for change.

Indeed, 1988 was a year of extensive health debate, as creation of the Prime Minister's review team encouraged almost every individual or institute that had ever made a policy suggestion on health – and even some that had not – to place in the public domain a scheme for NHS reform. Many options, it seemed, were open, though some institutes – such as the New Right think tanks Centre for Policy Studies (CPS), Adam Smith Institute (ASI) and Institute of Economic Affairs – were highly likely to gain a more sympathetic hearing from Thatcher and her advisers than were others.

In the event, the major proposal from the IEA, David Green's *Everyone a Private Patient*, stepped outside the consensus around the existing NHS funding regime which quickly emerged in the review team, and had little impact on *Working for Patients*. Far more influential were contributions from CPS and ASI authors. Indeed, there was a degree of common ground between the leading proposals put forward by these two institutes. Both Goldsmith and Willetts in *Managed Health Care*, written for the CPS, and Pirie and Butler in *The Health of Nations*, written for the ASI, came to the conclusion that some form of internal market in health care services should be created.

THE ROLES OF ENTHOVEN AND MAYNARD

Despite differences of emphasis, both pairs of authors sought to build on the work of American health care expert, Alain Enthoven. In 1985 Enthoven had developed the idea of an internal market in which health maintenance organisations (HMOs) with not less than 50 000 patients each would act as purchasers of health services from hospitals and other providers. With an important twist, this was the basic model favoured by the review team, among whom the late arrival as Health Secretary, Kenneth Clarke, was notably influential.

Enthoven thus pioneered the concept of the purchaser-provider distinction in the NHS, developing this notion during a research visit to the UK in the mid 1980s. Although his ideas were formally presented in a paper written for the Nuffield Provincial Hospitals Trust, they undoubtedly gained greater exposure from a lengthy feature in the *Economist* of 22 June 1985.

The important difference between Enthoven's plan and that which began to be implemented in 1991 lies entirely on the purchaser side of the internal market. Where Enthoven envisaged a necessary minimum of 50 000 patients per purchasing body, the GP fundholding practices which are now emerging in the NHS internal market operate at a minimum of less than 10 000 patients. Moreover, that minimum is being reduced by the year. As such, the internal market is much closer in conception to the ideas of British health care expert, Alan Maynard, who built on Enthoven's ideas to make the change from large to small purchasing bodies. Maynard is thought to have exercised a particularly strong influence on Clarke.

The importance of this difference to operation of the internal market is considered in later chapters. For now, the purchaser-provider distinction, which is central to both sets of reform proposals, is of more interest.

THE PURCHASER-PROVIDER DISTINCTION

The internal market reforms passed into law by means of the National Health Service and Community Care Act 1990. They were implemented – by gradualist means – from 1 April 1991. The key innovation made by them is the separation of purchasers from providers. It is from this measure that much else in the new NHS flows, for unless there is a clear division of purchasing and providing functions within the NHS, an internal market cannot operate. This fact was recognised by the Labour Party in its campaign against the present reforms, when it stated both in the 1992 election campaign and for many months beforehand that it would abolish the purchaser-provider distinction (and with it the very possibility of an internal market in the NHS).

The purchaser-provider distinction is straightforward. There are three types of purchaser of secondary care and community health services in the internal market. They are DHAs, GP fundholders, and private patients. There are also three types of provider of such care. They are NHS secondary care units (such as hospitals) which continue to be directly managed by their DHA (usually known as Directly Managed Units, or DMUs), NHS trusts, and private-sector units. Linking purchasers and providers is a series of contracts.

Two aspects of the NHS internal market are both novel and highly controversial. They are the new type of health care purchaser created by the reforms – the GP fundholder – and the new type of health care provider – the NHS trust. Each requires detailed consideration.

GP FUNDHOLDERS

A fundholding practice is one which controls its own budget, by means of which it both provides and buys a (limited) range of health care for its registered patients. This arrangement distinguishes it from a non-fundholding practice, which has secondary care bought on its behalf by a DHA.

This is a substantial difference. It allows a fundholding practice to shop around in the internal market for secondary patient care, instead of relying on purchasing decisions made by a DHA. However, it should be noted at the outset that there are limits to the extent of shopping around that even a GP fundholder can undertake. For the time being, the budget which practices handle covers only standard and inexpensive treatments. This is because two limitations have been imposed on practice spending by government. One is a list of permissible purchases outside of which practices cannot use their own budgets.[1] The other is a £5000 limit on practice liability for any one patient in a financial year. Once spending goes beyond this level, the DHA picks up the bill for treatment, thereby protecting fundholding practices against excessive expenditure on any one patient, and limiting potential risk.

The mechanism whereby a fundholding practice is created is simple. Should a general practice wish to become fundholding it makes an application to the relevant RHA, which will not approve practices with patient lists of less than a certain number of people. Initially, in April 1991, this number was set at 11 000. One year later, it was reduced to 9000. From April 1993 it will be 7000. Provided that they give due notice, practices which qualify for fundholder status can opt in or out of the new scheme at will. Thus far, only a few fundholding practices have sought to return to the old arrangements.

In the first wave, from 1 April 1991, 1720 GPs in 306 practices became fundholding. Although they represented only a small proportion of the 30 000 British GPs, they already covered 3.6 million people, or some 7.5 per cent of the British population. In the second wave, from 1 April 1992, a further 1400 GPs in 280 practices attained fundholder status, pushing the number of British people under the care of fundholding practices to 6.7 million, and the proportion to around 14 per cent. In the third wave, from 1 April 1993, 2500 GPs in more than 600 practices will join the scheme. Then, almost 25 per cent of the population will be registered with a fundholding practice.

By dividing the figure of 7000 by average GP list sizes, it is possible to determine how many GPs a practice must contain to meet one of the key criteria for fundholder status after April 1993. For more than a quarter of a century average list sizes have fallen throughout Britain, as GP numbers have risen. In England in December 1991, the average list size stood at 1887, such that English practices comprising four or more GPs can usually be expected to meet the key criterion for fundholding from April 1993. In other parts of Britain average list sizes are slightly smaller than in England – in Scotland, for example, they are just over 1500 – such that five GPs may be necessary before a practice reaches a combined list size of 7000. Nevertheless, fundholder status will soon be within the reach of many general practices.

Indeed, this point is reinforced by data relating to practice size. Table 5.1 reproduces statistics showing the number of GPs in England and Wales in practices of differing sizes.

Table 5.1: Distribution of GPs in England and Wales by practice size, 1988

Size of practice	Number of GPs
1	3050
2	4122
3	5049
4	4960
5	4140
6 or more	5600

Source: Connah and Pearson, op cit.

In 1988, a total of 12 221 GPs were in practices of three GPs or less, and 14 700 were in practices of four GPs or more. Provided that the distribution of GPs has not changed dramatically since 1988, the majority of GPs will be able to seek fundholder status from April 1993. Furthermore, through grouping or forming consortia with other practices, even small general practices can apply to become fundholding.

Once approval for fundholder status has been attained, practice budgets – which may now sometimes total more than £1 million – are deducted from the allocations of strategic authorities, and passed directly to the fundholding practice. They are calculated on the basis of three main expenditures faced by GPs: hospital and other secondary care services, practice staff and pharmaceuticals. The first of these three – hospital and other services – is deducted from the DHA's budget, and will eventually be determined strictly by the number of patients on a practice list, weighted by its age structure, its health profile, and the relative cost of providing care in the area in question. Currently, however, it is given a largely historical orientation: this aspect of a practice budget usually remains closely related to recent expenditure patterns. The final two of these three – practice staff and pharmaceuticals – are deducted from the budget of the relevant FHSA.

Three key freedoms which GP fundholders gain over non-fundholding practices are an ability to alter the mix between these three areas of expenditure, freedom to shop around for secondary care in the internal market, and the possibility of carrying savings – some might call them 'profits' – forward from one year to the next. 'Profits' cannot, however, be taken out of the practice and pocketed by the GPs involved in it (though they could conceivably be used to purchase various perks, such as travel to foreign conferences, and so on). Currently, fundholding practices are also given a special £16 000 start-up grant, and are awarded a £33 000 annual management fee. These terms are, however, starting to alter (for the worse) as more practices seek fundholder status.

Further advances in fundholding can nevertheless be expected in future years, as the government either reduces the minimum list size threshold still further, or encourages small practices to group together to secure fundholder status. GP fundholding could predominate in the primary sector towards the end of the 1990s.

NHS TRUSTS

NHS trusts are really the equivalent of GP fundholders in the acute sector of the NHS. To gain trust status, a hospital or other secondary care unit must be able to demonstrate financial health in the present and foreseeable future. On securing approval, NHS trusts opt out of DHA control, and become directly responsible to the Health Secretary. Like GP fundholders, 'opted-out' units are not privatised, but remain in the public sector as public corporations. They can opt back into DHA control, but none has yet chosen to do so.

There is, however, an important difference between the purchasing and providing sides of the new NHS. Whereas GP fundholders are fully funded by government for the range of primary care which they provide, NHS trusts (and, indeed, units which do not take trust status) are not. Each gets a block grant to cover core expenditures. In the case of units with trust status, this comes directly from the Department of Health. In the case of DMUs, it is passed from the Department to the DHA, and thence to the unit in question. All other income has, however, to be secured through competition for GP contracts.

Trust status confers important freedoms on a hospital or other secondary care unit, allowing it (within boundaries set by government) to specialise to a degree that is not possible at present, to have far greater autonomy in managing its assets, and to plough profits back into service improvements. Again, as the very status of a trust implies, no profits can be withdrawn from an NHS trust.

It is worth noting that although the idea of NHS trusts was originally developed as a model for acute hospital health care provision, it has in fact been extended well beyond this. In the very first wave, the full range of NHS patient services was represented in trust applications, stretching from community, mental handicap and mental health care to ambulance services.

This variegated pattern was reinforced in the second wave, when complex trust applications were made by consortia of different services. The six main types identified by Newchurch and Company, the leading consultancy firm to have emerged as a result of the development of NHS trusts, are:
- Acute services (the original model for NHS trusts)
- District provider units (an entire DHA which seeks to provide an integrated local health service in a single trust)
- Community and priority services
- Mental health and mental handicap services
- Specialist hospitals
- Ambulance services

In total, the first wave of applications saw 57 NHS trusts created out of the 66 which had applied for trust status. The hospitals in this first wave accounted for 41 000 beds out of an NHS total of nearly 300 000, and for more than 110 000 employees out of the one million or so who work for the NHS. The second wave saw a further 99 NHS trusts created, taking the total number of beds in NHS trusts to more than 120 000.

Further extensions of trust status are now highly probable. The total number of applicants for trust status in the third wave was 151. If, as seems likely, a large majority is approved by the Health Secretary, more than 200 000 hospital beds (more than two-thirds of the total) will be in NHS trusts from 1 April 1993. There is therefore a strong chance that trust status will be the predominant mode within the acute care sector from 1993, and possibly the unique mode from the middle of the present decade.

OPERATION OF THE INTERNAL MARKET

On both sides of the internal market, piecemeal creation of new institutions within the NHS means that funding increasingly by-passes the intermediate institutions (that is, the DHAs and FHSAs) created as part of the NHS planning system in 1974 and 1982, moving directly either from central government or from an RHA to the local level. There it 'follows the patient', for funding is now starting to move around the internal market according to purchasing decisions made on behalf of patients.

Indeed, the gradual emergence of a real market in hospital services is already visible in the development of pricing information. A new journal, *Fundholding*, launched in October 1991 quickly developed a directory of prices that GPs could expect to be quoted when shopping around for surgery. This list is not unlike the kind of information that could be advertised for routine car repairs. A specimen list of hospital prices is reproduced from *Fundholding* in Table 5.2 (overleaf).

Currently, however, separation of purchasers and providers in the internal market is not as clear and distinct as it is eventually likely to be. This is chiefly because the function of DHAs is anomalous. At present, they are responsible both for purchasing NHS care and for providing it. As purchasers, DHAs operate on behalf of GPs who have not (yet) chosen to seek fundholder status. As providers, they hold direct management responsibility for hospitals which have not (yet) chosen to seek trust status. In both cases, DHAs represent the vestiges of the old NHS. Even then their role is changing rapidly. On the hospital side, for example, they have already devolved a large amount of managerial responsibility to unit level, where general managers are in place. This anomaly is, then, temporary. It will be increasingly undermined as more and more GPs and hospitals opt out of direct FHSA or DHA control and into independent status within the internal market.

Table 5.2: Specimen list of hospital prices, South West Thames region, 1992

	Croydon £	East Surrey £	Kingston & Esher £	Merton & Sutton £	Mid- Downs £	Mid Surrey £
Total thyroidectomy	994	1715	1037	1160	1442	2139
Mastectomy	1628	1483	1285	1391	1251- 1643	1181
Salivary gland/ duct operations	369- 865	965- 1725	644- 1099	368- 1028	583- 1654	271- 1060
Total colectomy	3611- 4738	2466	2884	1688	2692- 4102	1761
Exteriorisation of bowel	3311- 3545	1671	2884	2893	2364- 2480	2592
Excision of rectum	3768	2638	2884	3206	2692- 2915	3874
Operations on the gall bladder	554- 2770	1825	2884	1358- 2101	1505- 2343	1768- 2587
Varicose vein stripping ligation	338- 510	903	644	368- 484	700- 806	533- 604
Repair of femoral hernia	1084- 1301	959	644	863- 1276	583- 700	407- 1301
Lymph node excision biopsy	586	914	644	1028	583- 1113	703

Note: All prices are quoted for inpatient surgery.
Source: *Fundholding*, 21 July 1992.

Eventually, the very great majority of funds should by-pass the intermediary institutions created by structural reforms in 1974 and 1982, as the great majority of general practices and NHS secondary care units opt out. The internal market will then be dominated by GP fundholders, and NHS trusts.

Competition is being encouraged on both sides of the internal market. Open registration provisions in the 1990 contract have increased competition amongst GPs for patients, and an increase in GP funds derived from capitation fees has made registrations a more important component of the total budget secured by a practice. To reinforce this shift towards a more competitive market for patients, GPs are now allowed to advertise. In the secondary care sector, both GP fundholders and DHAs are encouraged to shop around among hospitals in order to secure the best treatment for patients, in terms of both price and quality.

THE NEW CONTRACTUALISM

Tying the internal market together is a system of contracts. The NHS used to be funded uniquely as a provider of health care services: care would be provided either by a GP or by a consultant or nurse in a hospital, and money would be passed down the system to the unit that had incurred its cost. Now that the purchaser-provider distinction has been made, one half of the NHS will continue to be funded for the services which it provides, whilst the other half will be funded in order to purchase health care services. Crucially, however, the provider half of the NHS will have to compete in the internal market for the business of the purchaser half. No automatic funding for services rendered will be forthcoming. In these circumstances, the nature of contracts signed by purchasers and providers becomes crucial to NHS development.

Three basic types of contract are envisaged:
- Block contracts, whereby access to a specified range of services is purchased in advance of service delivery. Under this arrangement, purchasers do not buy, say, 100 operations of a certain kind, but the possibility of sending for treatment any patient who needs an operation during the period of time covered by the contract. The outturn might be more or less treatment than was originally envisaged when the contract was signed (and would presumably thereby determine the terms of the next year's contract).
- Cost and volume contracts, whereby a set of charges for a given number of courses of treatment is agreed. Under this arrangement, purchasers buy, say, up to 100 specified operations at £1000 each, falling to £800 each if more than 100 operations are purchased.
- Cost per case contracts, whereby a set of charges per individual case is set.

The new contractualism which is established at the heart of the internal market is a major and key innovation. It substantially extends the cultural shift towards business practices which was made with the introduction of general management in 1984, and places a key discipline on (some) medical professionals. It is also an inherent aspect of the new NHS.

PARALLEL CHANGES IN COMMUNITY CARE

It is worth noting that parallel changes are currently being made in the field of community care. In the past, such care was directly funded and provided by the state sector, though there was a division of function between the Department of Social Security and local authorities. However, from the mid 1980s this system was subjected to sustained criticism, notably by parliamentary select committees, and by the Audit Commission, which was particularly scathing in its assessment of existing arrangements. The result was a second Griffiths report, *Agenda for Action*, presented to the Secretary of State in March 1988, and an important White Paper, *Caring for People*, published in November 1989.

The controversial aspect of Griffiths' second report was the proposal that local authorities be given the key purchaser role in a community care market within which a wide variety of providers would operate (on the same principle as the NHS internal market). The Thatcher administration not being known for the respect and trust it accorded local authorities, this was always likely to be a recommendation which would face strong political opposition at the highest level.

However, the logic of Griffiths' argument eventually won the day, and an only slightly diluted version of his proposals appeared in the White Paper. It duly passed into law alongside the NHS internal market reforms in the National Health Service and Community Care Act 1990. Implementation of the new system was, however, caught and held up in the problems created by community charge (or poll tax) in 1990, and the target start date was shifted from 1 April 1991 to 1 April 1993.

Once the new system has been fully implemented it will mirror that created in the NHS, with one important difference. This is that greater strategic capacity will be generated by the fact that purchasers will have the size of a local authority, rather than merely that of a fundholding general practice. The parallel between the two new systems would be much closer if DHAs, rather than GP fundholders, had been made the key purchaser institutions within the NHS. In the field of community care, then, each responsible local authority (currently county councils and metropolitan districts) will employ care managers to take responsibility for assessing care needs and purchasing care. This, too, is a system which is only now being created.

Although no attempt has yet been made to integrate health and community care, the present parallel reform processes make this a future possibility. With the separation of purchaser and provider functions, it becomes feasible to fuse health and community care purchasing roles in an integrated structure.

A SELF-INVENTING SYSTEM

The NHS internal market is, then, currently under construction. It is important to note that the very big structural change which it involves is not being imposed from the top, as was the case with the 1974 and 1982 reorganisations. Instead, what has happened is that government has altered incentive structures within the NHS as a means of encouraging change from the bottom. GPs can gain autonomy, status and the odd financial reward (such as substantial grants towards the cost of new computer systems) if they opt to become fundholders. Similarly, hospitals and other parts of the secondary care sector can gain independence and become self-governing units able to set their own priorities if they opt for trust status.

The new NHS is a self-inventing system.[2] The Conservatives' 1992 election victory, and the many incentives which are offered to general practices and units in the secondary sector to take fundholding and trust status, mean that it is likely to invent itself with considerable speed.

NOTES

1. This list is reproduced in the appendix to H Glennerster, M Matsaganis and P Owens, *A Foothold for Fundholding: A Preliminary Report on the Introduction of GP Fundholding* (King's Fund Institute, London, 1992). A full discussion of fundholding may also be found in this publication.
2. P Day and R Klein, 'The Politics of Modernization: Britain's National Health Service in the 1980s', *Milbank Quarterly* 67 (1989), 1-34.

6 THE NHS IN THE 1990s

Two separate reform programmes are feeding through the NHS at present. One is the shift to general management, pursued since 1984. The other is the internal market initiative, launched on a gradualist basis in 1991. Together, they will have a major impact on the NHS of the 1990s.

THE TWO REFORM PROGRAMMES CONTRASTED

It is important to begin by reviewing the distinct dynamics of the two reform programmes. The shift to general management sought increased efficiency and cost effectiveness in the NHS through creation of a clear managerial hierarchy. This is now in place, and stretches from the Policy Board and Management Executive down through RHAs to DHAs and FHSAs and, finally, to hospitals, GPs and other bodies which operate at the base of the NHS. Within this hierarchy, the operational importance of the NHS Management Executive is substantial. Many directives issued by health authorities emanate from it. This is, then, essentially a regulatory dynamic.

The internal market initiative has an entirely different dynamic. It also seeks increased efficiency and cost effectiveness in the NHS – though it has other aims too, such as increased choice for consumers of health care services – but it does so by means of competitive pressures. The whole thrust of the internal market programme is to generate within the NHS the kinds of disciplines on medical behaviour which exist in competitive markets for other goods and services. It is therefore a dynamic of fragmentation and release into a competitive market.

It is evident that these two dynamics are distinct. Where the Griffiths reforms had sought to turn the NHS into an efficient but still unified business, the internal market reforms seek to split the NHS into efficient and competitive units. Efficiency thus remains a central objective, but it will now be generated not by an efficient monolith, but by the most efficient units in an internal market. Other policy objectives – such as increased choice – are also expected to flow from the marketisation reforms of the 1990s.

The key point to be made here is that these two very different dynamics currently coexist in the NHS. Even as the internal market reforms are in the process of implementation, regulatory mechanisms continue to be strengthened. Indeed, the control exercised by the NHS Management Executive is probably greater now than it has ever been. In these circumstances, the impact of reform on the NHS of the 1990s is genuinely difficult to predict.

POSSIBLE IMPACTS

In a strongly regulated health care system in which creation of autonomous units is nevertheless in process, and fragmentation is therefore a reality, several outcomes are feasible. The NHS of the 1990s could move in one of four main directions.

First, it could be genuinely fragmented into a series of market-level units which are regulated, but in no sense directed, by upper tiers of the NHS hierarchy. This could properly be described as a marketised system.

Fragmentation could, however, be counteracted in one of three main ways, which provide the other main directions in which the NHS of the 1990s could move. First, consortia of purchasers could emerge to generate local or regional monopolies of demand. Secondly, consortia of providers could emerge to generate local or regional monopolies of supply. Thirdly, the entire system of fragmentation could in effect be rendered nugatory by central intervention on both sides of the internal market which stretched far beyond mere regulation to become direction and control.

It might be noted that real fragmentation would be a very radical departure from existing arrangements. Should fragmentation be counteracted in one of the three possible ways listed above, the new NHS of the 1990s would, however, be less different from the old NHS of the years up to 1991.

EARLY INDICATIONS OF CHANGE

Early indications of change are hard to read. This is because fragmentation into opted-out units is taking place only gradually. More generally, an internal market for health care services is only developing slowly. Indeed, the government decreed that Year 1 (April 1991 – April 1992) should be a 'steady state', in which no really radical changes in either purchasing or provision of health care services should take place, and that Year 2 should differ from it only incrementally in being a period of 'managed change'.

Thus far, the government's wishes have been respected, and no radical transformation of NHS procedures has yet taken place. This has not simply been the result of spontaneous conformity on the part of opted-out (and other) units in the new NHS. Instead, behind much present behaviour may be found the strong directive power of the NHS Management Executive. An evolving regional dimension to the Management Executive makes this power all the more formidable.

The key question is whether NHS procedures will ever be radically transformed. Clearly the important structural and cultural shift to a marketised system is being made, and it can only be a matter of time before some of the consequences of this shift feed through into NHS operations. However, the fact that strong regulatory bodies remain in place means that the exact nature of the regulated market which will emerge in the NHS is open to debate.

THE DYNAMIC OF PURCHASERS AND PROVIDERS

To tackle this question, it is necessary to analyse in some detail the dynamic of purchasers and providers. It cannot be stated too often that this dynamic is the defining characteristic of the Conservatives' internal market programme. Separation of purchasers from providers within the NHS makes the internal market possible. Much else therefore flows from it.

In the present reform programme, the change which has perhaps caused greatest disquiet among the British public is trust status for NHS hospitals. Charges of privatisation tend to focus on trust status in the acute sector, and allegations of underfunding are targeted most easily and clearly on closed hospital wards or non-existent acute services. The media copy provided by such aspects of the reform programme is irresistible.

However, this disquiet is only valid if the provider side of the internal market turns out to provide its central dynamic. To determine whether this is likely to be so, it is necessary to analyse the kinds of market relations which will emerge as the reform process develops and the internal market gradually frees itself from the many non-market relations which currently structure it.

It is quite possible that hospitals will indeed develop covert or possibly even overt consortia which transform the supply side of the internal market from an essentially competitive arena into one which is oligopolistic, duopolistic or even monopolistic. Should this happen, GP fundholders and any remaining DHAs will be forced into the position of price takers, unable to use their purchasing power to influence either the price or the quality of the services their patients consume.

In markets for routine operations (such as hernias, hip replacements, mastectomies and the like), which form the core of treatments for which GP fundholders are currently allowed to shop around, such a development seems improbable. It is certainly not visible at present, as was demonstrated by the range of prices quoted in Table 5.2. Furthermore, it is likely to be outlawed by government should signs of its happening emerge. The probability of competition among providers of routine and inexpensive treatments is therefore high. In this sector, competition is moreover likely to operate over quite a large geographical area. GP fundholders already have access to extensive pricing guides which allow them to make precise and informed assessments of the range of secondary health care services available in their locality. Should a nearby hospital quote high prices for routine operations, a purchaser could threaten to switch business to more distant providers. Such a threat could also be carried out, for GPs are likely to have little difficulty in persuading patients that their needs will be better served in a distant rather than a local hospital.

Yet this still leaves a large number of hospital services for which there is currently little competitive demand. These are either non-routine, or breach the £5000 limit imposed on fundholder purchases and are therefore made by DHAs on behalf of all GPs, whether fundholding or not. It is true that DHAs are themselves starting to shop around, but the competitive pressure which they are likely to exert on the secondary care sector remains limited. Across a large range of secondary care, the internal market could therefore become provider-driven.

In these circumstances, it is probable that a hybrid situation will emerge in which monopoly of supply (in some markets) coexists with substantial amounts of competition (in others). This may provide conditions in which government is able to exercise a significant controlling function over a very wide area. However, it is unlikely to allow central direction of the NHS to be in any sense total. This is because GP fundholders are a genuinely unpredictable element in the new NHS. Monopoly of demand and supply in all health care markets is rendered improbable by their institution, as is effective government control of the entire NHS. In the new NHS, a key dynamic will rest with the many thousands of fundholding practices which are certain to emerge in the course of the 1990s.

For this reason, a focus of public concern on trust status in the hospital sector is perhaps misplaced. The radical changes are taking place in the primary care sector. In the internal market, a number of health care outcomes will therefore be demand-driven. Should pluralism of supply emerge – as seems likely for routine, inexpensive treatments – the secondary care sector will develop elements of genuine competition, and prices faced by customers will be driven down. In strategic terms, the purchaser side of the internal market is crucial to change in the increasingly marketised NHS.

THE REALITY OF FRAGMENTATION

The likely extent of fragmentation of the NHS in the 1990s should not be exaggerated. Many mechanisms still exist whereby not just regulation, but also direction and control of Britain's health care system can be exercised by strategic tiers of authority. As has already been stated, the growing power of the NHS Management Executive is notable in this regard, particularly as it is currently being reinforced by a new regional presence.

Moreover, pressure to place limits on fragmentation is highly likely to remain substantial throughout the 1990s. This is partly because governments in the 1990s, as in all decades since World War Two, will be held responsible by the British people for health care provision, and will therefore seek to counteract the more unpopular consequences of fragmentation. Indeed, such action was viewed in the very early stages of GP fundholding. When, in 1991, it became apparent that some fundholding practices were attempting to use their purchasing power to circumvent hospital waiting lists, government moved quickly to prevent this from happening. A further reason why central attempts to direct health care outcomes can be expected to remain substantial in the 1990s relates to the *Patient's Charter* initiative. By setting targets for a range of health care services – in particular, for reductions in waiting lists for hospital treatment – the *Charter* significantly increases the determination of government to ensure that the NHS performs in line with its stated objectives.[1]

Yet even developed pressures on government to retain control of the NHS are likely to be no more than partially effective in much of the primary care sector. Although government has many reasons to seek control, it nevertheless seems improbable that fundholder autonomy will continue to be substantially limited as the 1990s progress and the extent of fundholding develops. With time, GP fundholders can instead be expected to act increasingly to undermine strategic priorities developed by health authorities. In consequence, primary care provision will be substantially diversified away from needs-based assessments towards a more market-driven distribution.

Limits to fragmentation will certainly be present in the new NHS, but they are highly unlikely to be total. This is because of the unpredictability which GP fundholding represents. In this part of the new NHS, it is difficult to envisage ways in which the consequences of fragmentation could be wholly overcome.

THE IMPACT ON PRIMARY CARE

The impact of reform on primary care is, then, key to NHS development in the 1990s. Here, as in the secondary care sector, mechanisms of both regulation and marketisation are currently being instituted. Regulatory measures comprise limits on prescribable drugs, the imposition of indicative amounts, targets for preventive care, and minimum standards provisions written into the 1990 contract. They were analysed in Chapter 2. The competitive dynamic remains to be investigated here.

It is important to separate two distinct aspects of the more competitive environment in which GPs currently find themselves. One is increased competition for patients. This change was made by the 1990 contract, which raised capitation payments, sanctioned advertisement by GPs, and made provisions for open registration. Its effect has been to increase pressure on GPs to offer a high level of patient service. Should they fail to do so, patients are now able to switch to another practice with some ease, taking their capitation payments with them.

The other aspect of the more competitive environment in which GPs now find themselves is a product of the internal market reforms themselves. This is the ability to shop around in the internal market for (some) secondary care. It is, however, secured only by GP fundholders. Non-fundholders continue to have hospital treatment bought on their behalf by a DHA, which will certainly consult with practices for which it is making purchases but will nevertheless itself exercise the final power of decision.

The impact of increased competition among GPs for patients is therefore the more widespread of the two. Many practices, whether fundholding or not, are now making considerable innovations to the range of GP services historically made available to the British public. Some have opened minor operations theatres and are able to perform operations on their practice premises which formerly would have been referred automatically to the local hospital. In offering these new practice-based services, GPs are sometimes employing hospital consultants to travel to their surgeries (rather than obliging patients to travel to consultants in hospitals). Desk-top pathology is also being substantially developed by a number of practices.

Among fundholders, the mix of secondary care which is purchased, and the hospitals with which contracts are signed, are gradually changing. It must, however, be noted that current limitations on fundholder purchasing mean that even these practices only purchase a small amount – perhaps 10 or 20 per cent – of secondary care themselves, the remainder still being bought for them by a DHA. The discretionary nature of fundholder purchases does, however, increase their importance.

The impact on primary care is currently limited. Nevertheless, the fact that the advantages of competition are secured primarily by fundholding practices – in terms of increases in choice, freedom and reward – means that fundholder status is being sought by more and more general practices. As their numbers grow, fundholding practices will exert increasing pressure for change on the way in which the NHS operates. At this point, the limits of government regulation will be tested.

An important consequence of purchaser power in the new NHS is that it increases the importance of those GPs which take fundholder status. GPs have always played an important role in the NHS, acting since its creation as gatekeepers to hospital services. In Britain, access to the central and most expensive part of the health care system – consultants in hospitals

– is controlled by GPs. To this traditional function, the internal market adds a new one. As well as being gatekeepers GPs will now act as purchasing agents on behalf of their patients. As such, they will gain significant power within the NHS, for through the placing (or non-placing) of contracts they will be able to determine winners and losers among hospitals competing for business in the internal market.

Indeed, for the first time the substantial consultant power created by institution of the NHS in 1948 will come under serious attack. In the old NHS consultants formed the central power bloc, being providers of prestigious acute services for which GPs became something akin to supplicants. Under the new system, GPs have gained the crucial power of funding those services, and are no longer in the position of supplicants, but of highly-valued customers. As such, their wishes will be accorded a great deal more attention than was previously the case.

The key aspect of the new-style fundholding GP which needs to be emphasised here is the market-level competence to take decisions on a patient's behalf which is created by the NHS reforms. The old NHS operated almost as a transmission belt of health care, transferring patients almost automatically from GP to the local hospital if further treatment were required. In the new NHS, GPs will be able to take a wider view of their own patients' needs, and to decide which among a variety of hospitals is likely to provide the best care in the circumstances.

In this way, the medical definition of disease, centred on 'glamour' services provided by hospital consultants, may well come under close scrutiny and challenge as a transfer of emphasis from secondary to primary care takes place. The automaticity of the transmission belt which operated under the old system will be greatly reduced. In the internal health market which is currently being created, GPs acting as purchasers will be an important driving force.

THE IMPACT ON SECONDARY CARE

In the secondary sector, control and competition are also evident. Control is being increased by means of clinical audit, which is increasingly subjecting consultants to peer review, and related accountability mechanisms. Incentives to compete in the internal market are very strong for all units. Unless they secure contracts for health care they will go out of business.

The increased specialisation which is already evident in the secondary care sector is one pointer to the future. Indeed, as the 1990s progress, hospitals (and other parts of this sector) can be expected to take one of two routes. Either they will specialise in hi-tech areas of treatment in which they have particular skills (or, in business jargon, possess a competitive advantage), or they will become low-tech, low-cost hospitals offering cheap, routine treatments. The old general hospital which offered a broad range of acute treatments will become increasingly rare, though some regulation of change in this regard is being conducted by government.

Beyond this, closures, takeovers and mergers will increase markedly. Indeed, the initial controversies which arose with regard to the internal market reforms concerned job losses in trust hospitals and threats to a series of prestigious London hospitals. In each case, these issues are indications of future trends.

The issue of job losses was initially raised by two hospital trusts created in the first wave. Immediately after trust status had been secured in April 1991 job cuts of 600 were announced at Guy's in south London (where a deficit of £6.8 million was revealed), and of 300 at Bradford Royal. Despite Labour Party and BMA pressure, Health Secretary William Waldegrave stuck to the principles of the new system by refusing to intervene in either case. He insisted, moreover, that hospital trusts would continue to be created. A similar government line has been taken on subsequent announcements of job cuts.

A far larger, and in some ways related, controversy is building over the future of health care in London. Currently, London's health services are 20 per cent more expensive than are those in other parts of the country. However, this figure for the entire metropolis masks a situation of near-equality between outer London and the rest of England, and a corresponding differential of 45 per cent between inner London and the English average. Inner London has more hospitals, and therefore more consultants, than anywhere else in Britain. Its GP and community services are, however, among the worst in the country, for overfunding of prestigious teaching hospitals has as its counterpart underfunding of more humdrum medical services.

With the introduction of weighted capitation funding, the amount of health spending taken by London will certainly fall dramatically. Indeed, the shift to the new funding system has been delayed in an explicit attempt to reduce the drama of its impact on London. In the end, however, the new system will undoubtedly be introduced, even if some of its terms are modified slightly. When this happens, London hospitals will only be able to survive by the same means open to all other NHS hospitals (whether they have trust status or not): successful competition in the internal market. High fixed (London capital charges) and variable (London salaries) costs mean that not all hospitals will manage to do this.

The certain consequence is that hospitals in London will close. A report, *London Health Care 2010*, published by the independent King's Fund Commission on the Future of London's Acute Services in June 1992, put the required number of closures at 15 (out of 41 acute London hospitals with more than 250 beds). In total, some 7000 beds could be lost. The highly probable consequence is that some of the closures will be famous teaching hospitals. In July 1992 it was reported – and denied – that the South East Thames RHA had decided that either or Guy's (which has trust status) or St Thomas's should be closed as part of a rationalisation of inner London hospital services. Other prestigious hospitals will undoubtedly be threatened with closure in years to come. The possible benefit is that more funding will flow to London's GP and community services.

A government review of London's health services, due for publication in autumn 1992, is likely to reach precisely these sorts of conclusions. They will be implemented by a special task force set up by the Health Department (in line with King's Fund recommendations). By the year 2010 to which the King's Fund Commission looked, London will have fewer hospitals, fewer consultants, fewer junior doctors and fewer medical students. If all goes to plan it will also have better GP and community services. As such, its health care provisions should begin to resemble those in the rest of the country.

The likely impact of internal market reforms on London's health services is, however, no more than an extreme case of more general changes which will sweep the NHS in the course of the 1990s. In many parts of Britain, hospitals will close and bed numbers will be reduced. Indeed, this reflects a secular trend in mature health care systems throughout the world, all of which face a major problem of over-provision of hospital beds. As modern technology reduces the need for in-patient care, so hospitals are becoming increasingly redundant. In the NHS over the past 20 years the number of hospitals providing acute care has fallen by 30 per cent, and the total number of beds in those hospitals has fallen by 25 per cent. It might be noted that the same 20 years have seen the number of people treated in each bed almost double to 40 per year.[2]

Peripheral innovation is also likely. Indeed, such innovation has already been witnessed in initiatives such as the opening of the UK's first patient hotel at Kingston Hospital Trust in August 1991.

THE NEW CONTRACTUALISM IN OPERATION

Gradual development of the internal market has caused, contracts and price lists also to develop. In line with government desire for a 'steady state' in the internal market's first year, most initial contracts reflected historical patterns of health care delivery, and were close to block contracts simply covering a similar package of services to those consumed in the previous year. Little shopping around took place.

This was, in fact, just as well, because few hospitals – whether they had trust status or not – had much idea in the first year of how to price their services in terms of individual operations or treatments. The result was substantial anomalies in price.

Similarly, the variation in fundholding practice budgets in the first year of the internal market was also marked. Fundholding budgets in three health regions studied by Day and Klein averaged £109 per patient. Yet the outlying points in their survey were £52 and £176 per patient (a differential of precisely three times).[3]

Such substantial variations as these will certainly be reduced as the internal market settles into full operation. It is important to note that these variations are not however the product of the internal market. They have simply been revealed by its creation. Just as the RAWP formula of 1976 revealed big regional and local variations in health service spending, so the internal market reforms are making variations in cost per episode of health care evident. However, having been brought into the open, they are likely to be rapidly reduced. On the purchaser side this will be the result of political pressure for equalisation of resource distribution. On the provider side it will be the result of competitive pressures. Unless hospitals and other units can compete in the internal market, they will gain no health care business from purchasers.

However, it is not only on price that hospitals are competing for business. Increasingly, purchasers are demanding that minimum levels of service – in terms of standards of care and quality – are written into contracts. In future it is likely that the problem of waiting lists will indeed be tackled by this mechanism, with purchasers insisting that certain treatments be delivered within a specified time period, and perhaps being prepared to pay a premium for it.

THE IMPACT OF THE NEW CONTRACTUALISM

A generalised change which is involved in the move from old to new NHS is the fundamental shift from relationships based on trust to ones based on contract. It is important not to exaggerate the speed or extent of this change. At least in the short term a considerable amount of trust built up under the old NHS will continue to pervade the new system. Moreover, to the degree that professional standards remain defining features of the new NHS, trust will continue to be a key component of its internal relations.

Yet by the same token the magnitude of this change should not be dismissed. The new NHS, based on a system of contracts, is very different from the NHS which was created in 1948. This operated in a collegiate and professional manner, until it was subjected to managerial reform in the 1980s. Development of the internal market is currently reinforcing the 1980s paradigm shift to business practices in a very significant way. Precise specification of terms and conditions is becoming more important than ever it was in the past, and a more businesslike orientation is gradually spreading through the NHS. Reinforcement of this change is inherent in the internal market reforms themselves, and will develop largely independently of the battle for control waged by purchasers and providers.

THE CHANGING ROLES OF DHAs AND RHAs

In the internal market growing numbers of GPs are acquiring control over their own budgets through fundholder status, and more and more hospitals and other units in the secondary sector are being funded directly by the Department of Health through trust status. In consequence the roles of strategic health authorities are changing dramatically. From a position in the old NHS in which they took strategic health decisions on behalf of the populations they served, DHAs and RHAs are increasingly finding themselves unable to take such choices because the cash through which strategic priorities might be pursued is no longer in their control.

One consequence of the slow haemorrhage of funds from strategic authorities to GP fundholders is that DHAs are now combining to form purchasing consortia to act on behalf of the declining numbers of GPs who are not yet fundholders (and who therefore have services bought on their behalf by DHAs). Yet in the long term, as more and more GPs take fundholder status, even these consortia will dwindle in size and importance.

In these circumstances, DHAs and RHAs are likely to take on entirely new roles, and to act as local and regional regulators in a decentralised NHS. RHAs are particularly well suited to this task, for it will be some years yet before DHAs find themselves entirely freed from operating in the internal market and in a position to regulate it. RHAs, by contrast, are well placed to regulate the new market for health care, and to act as arbitrators in contractual disputes between purchasers and providers. This role of court of appeal can be expected to become the main function of RHAs by the end of the century.

It is, by contrast, difficult to judge how strategic decisions embodied in health needs assessment exercises will continue to be made by health authorities. Whilst health authorities will no doubt continue to plan Britain's health care arrangements, they will increasingly find that those plans are undermined by the activities of GP fundholders in the internal market.

NEW FUNCTIONS AT THE CENTRE

The traditional functions carried out by central government institutions have been strategic, involving overall planning of health care provision. However, the point about GP fundholders applies here, as elsewhere: that if some health care outcomes become demand-driven, and purchasing power is placed in the hands of GPs, then strategic functions are substantially undermined. In these circumstances, the character of central government institutions is also likely to change in line with the dynamics of the new NHS.

Nevertheless, certain strategic functions could – and indeed are likely to – continue to be carried out by central bodies such as the Policy

Board and the Management Executive. This is partly because the ultimate distributor of health service funding is the government, which in consultation and joint action with RHAs is likely to set health priorities for the entire nation. It is also because the new NHS will remain highly political, and will therefore need to respond to political imperatives which will, again, be fixed at the top.

Central direction could operate in a number of ways. One possibility is that the customary British use of government circulars instructing GPs to devote more resources to areas of particular concern could be extended from the old NHS to the new. However, it is likely that GPs who are concerned about the use they make of their own budgets, and who are increasingly militant in defence of their acquired autonomy, will become ever less amenable to direction in this way. More likely, then, is that government – and RHAs – will increasingly resort to distributing ring-fenced grants which can only be spent on precisely identified initiatives. Indeed, this practice has existed for a long time, with special funds having been created in recent years to deal with such matters as AIDS, breast screening services and the continuing waiting list problem. In this way, an element of strategic capacity will be retained by the upper tiers of the new NHS. It is, however, likely to be less substantial than that which exists currently.

SHIFTING THE BALANCE WITHIN THE INTERNAL MARKET

The internal market reforms entail, therefore, a shift of balance within the NHS. The crucial change derives from the separation of purchaser and provider functions. This introduces an entirely new dynamic into the NHS and gives it a market orientation which it has never before possessed. Much of the drive in the new NHS is now bottom-up rather than top-down. However, top-down capacity within the NHS has not been completely undermined, as any government which is held to political account for the NHS can be expected to want to exercise significant amounts of control over it.

Indeed, the tension between independent units operating with substantial amounts of autonomy at the base of the Service, and ministers seeking to retain significant amounts of control at the top, is central to the new NHS. It is in many ways latent at present, because the internal market is only in its infancy. It will soon emerge, however, as the major determinant of the nature of the new NHS.

Resolution of this tension can only take place in one of two ways. One is that autonomy at the base will be severely limited, and control in the NHS will continue to reside chiefly at the centre. This will happen if the present attempt to release government ministers from political responsibility for the NHS fails to convince the British public. Despite similar feats having been accomplished in several policy domains through privatisation in the 1980s, such a possibility apparently remains distant in health. Popular commitment to a national service is still substantial.

The other is that autonomy at the base will be fully exploited, and a fragmented NHS will duly be created. Today, such a scenario seems incredible, yet it is the real logic of the internal market reforms. Furthermore, there is in reality little to stop it happening. Should GP fundholders – which are the key institution in the new NHS – exercise the autonomy which is currently being allowed them, strategic tiers in the NHS will be increasingly undermined. It is currently unclear how FHSAs will seek – or manage – to direct fundholder behaviour in areas in which it is now allowed free rein.

It is important to stress that formal regulation is not the key issue here. Undoubtedly the NHS internal market will always be regulated, as are virtually all British markets. What it will increasingly lack is strategic direction towards a series of health priorities which can only be set at upper levels of the NHS. It is in this sense that fragmentation through the internal market reforms poses a threat to the historic functioning of the NHS.

NOTES

1. C Paton, 'Firm Control', *Health Service Journal*, 6 August 1992, 20-2.
2. B Connah and R Pearson, *NHS Handbook*, 7th ed. (NAHAT/Macmillan, London, 1991).
3. P Day and R Klein, 'Variations in Budgets of Fund-Holding Practices', *British Medical Journal* 303 (1991), 168-70.

7 STRENGTHS AND WEAKNESSES OF A MARKETISED NHS

The new NHS is currently being created through progressive fragmentation and disintegration of the old. In the process, a new set of internal dynamics is being established in Britain's health care system as the balance of power within that system shifts. Distinctive strengths and weaknesses are generated by marketisation.

STRENGTHS AND WEAKNESSES OF THE OLD NHS

At the start of any assessment of strengths and weaknesses of the new NHS, it is worth briefly reviewing strengths and weaknesses of the old. There is always a temptation to idealise the old NHS, and to praise its egalitarian provision of health care through a unified system. Yet the NHS never did deliver equality of access – indeed, the Black Report of 1980 claims that it increased inequalities in this regard – and it never was unified.

The real strengths of the old NHS were public commitment to the ideals for which it stood, and widespread belief that it came tolerably close to achieving them. Each was, however, a wasting asset. Beyond this, the NHS was certainly inexpensive, and in many ways effective. The primary weakness of the old NHS was its inability to meet changing public demands in the sphere of health care. On the one hand, such demands expressed a desire for increased individual control of health care. On the other, they registered frustration with NHS responsiveness. This was expressed most dramatically in the linked waiting list and underfunding crises which prompted major review of the system in the late 1980s, and reform in 1991. This is nevertheless an impressive balance of strengths and weaknesses. It sets high standards for the new NHS.

FROM PATERNALISM TO AUTONOMY

One major advantage of the new NHS identified by government ministers is the replacement of health service paternalism by a system in which individual choice and autonomy are greatly increased. An important question is, however, whether clear increases in autonomy on the purchaser side of the internal market will be secured by individual patients, or by the GPs who advise them and act on their behalf.

The answer is that it will in fact be divided between them. On the one hand, open registration and expanded public information services embodied in the 1990 contract increase competition among GPs and make it a great deal easier for individuals to switch practices should they be dissatisfied with the service which they currently receive. Increases in capitation payments reinforce this change by giving GPs every incentive to register new patients. On the other, GPs will always need to act as important advisers to patients, and will continue to take decisions on their behalf, simply because they are more informed and expert in health care matters.

As far as the individual patient is concerned, the new NHS therefore generates a move from paternalism to autonomy which is real, but not complete. However, it is both undesirable and impossible to make a complete transition in this regard. Gains registered by GP fundholders will possibly be greater still. They are being set up as key purchasers of health care in the internal market, yet also remain substantial providers of services in their own right. Indeed, only a very small proportion – some 7 per cent – of GP consultations result in referral for further treatment outside the GP's competence.

In the internal market, as GPs' competence increases, so the number of treatments which are referred beyond the practice will diminish. In these circumstances an important series of fundholding power bases, on which the pressure of market forces may only be slight, will be created. Only government regulation may act as a real disciplinary force. A marketised NHS will shift power to the purchaser side of the internal market. To ensure that at least some of it reaches individual patients, close attention will have to be paid to GP fundholder activity.

AN INCREASE IN RESPONSIVENESS?

It is possible that the new NHS will be more responsive than was the old. This is because new pricing arrangements which lie at the heart of the internal market and which will act as an important determinant of service provision substantially increase the visibility of NHS operations. Instead of health care provision being decided on a strategic basis by NHS planners, it will increasingly be determined by the purchasing decisions of GP fundholders.

This in fact places the new visibility of NHS operations at one remove from the general public which is the primary judge of NHS responsiveness. However, there is no reason to suppose that GPs will not seek to enlist public support for increases in service funding of which they are aware. In this way, an important alliance could develop between GPs and patients in an attempt to squeeze more resources out of an ever-reluctant government. The development of quasi-market relations, and the pricing information they generate, seem likely to make the new NHS more responsive than was the old.

THE ISSUE OF EFFICIENCY

Underpinning many claims made for the new NHS is the increased efficiency which will be generated by it. About this issue, as about many others, it is however difficult to make a conclusive judgment. To the extent to which the internal market becomes purchaser-driven, supplier prices should be forced down by the pressure of competition, and efficiency gains should be registered. In short, efficiency of hospital provision should be increased by purchaser power. In the primary sector, the provision for GP fundholders to retain any savings made across the accounting year should also promote efficiency gains. In this case, however, they will not necessarily issue in lower overall costs, but may be used to increase service levels. This remains an important efficiency gain.

Within the issue of efficiency, there is, however, the issue of potential administrative explosion. A concern provoked by the new system is that it will substantially increase administrative costs in the NHS. Indeed, when William Waldegrave was Health Secretary he acknowledged that health authorities would spend in the region of £300 million on new administrative costs in the first year of internal market operation. These were partly one-off costs of getting the new system off the ground, but mainly costs which will be incurred throughout the lifetime of the internal market.

Establishing the extent to which this represents an administrative 'explosion' is extremely difficult. As has already been noted, the first-wave of GP fundholders covered only 7.5 per cent of the British population, and NHS trusts numbered only 57. This suggests that £300 million is an extremely large administrative burden. Multiplied up, it comes to several billions of pounds for a fully opted-out NHS. However, not all of the £300 million was spent by fundholders and units with trust status, but went instead on new computing systems at DHA and FHSA level. It is therefore highly likely that many of these costs are fixed and would not be incurred in full with every new wave of fundholding and trust status. In these circumstances, assessing the administrative consequences of reform is best attempted only in the abstract.

When this is done, it becomes clear that new administrative costs must be incurred by the development of contractualism. However, it may well be that old administrative burdens will also be lost as existing health authority bureaucracy is cut. The two processes could simply cancel each other out. Beyond this, it can be argued that efficiency gains under the new system will easily cover any additional administrative burden which may be generated. Furthermore, many of these gains are strictly unattainable in the absence of the improved pricing information which development of the internal market entails.

FROM NEED TO DEMAND

Against possible and likely strengths of the new NHS must be set a number of weaknesses. One which will only emerge if the internal market does indeed become purchaser-driven is a switch from need to demand as the main determinant of health outcomes.

In the old NHS access to health care was regulated centrally and regionally, and administered locally. This does not mean that there were not substantial differences in access to care. As has already been noted, the Black Report of 1980 found significant variations between socio-economic groups, the well-off and articulate securing more benefit from the NHS (and, indeed, the welfare state in general) than the poor and disadvantaged. It does mean that within the NHS the fiction of equal access was maintained. No top-up payments for premium service were allowed, and access was widely believed to be socially just, at least in an approximate sense.

In the new NHS this situation is fundamentally altered. The old unitary system is fragmented into a series of independent and autonomous agents by creation of GP fundholders. This fragmentation has a number of consequences. First, in an important psychological sense it undermines the notion of a unified Service. Second, in a practical sense it reinforces this by licensing GP fundholders to make innovations in primary care. Third, in consequence it substantially increases the likelihood

of diversity in primary care. A shift in criteria by which health care is allo-
cated – from need to demand – is the probable result.

By this is meant that aggregate health outcomes will in future be
determined more by the many purchasing decisions taken by GP
fundholders in the internal market than by the sorts of strategic
assessments of need taken in the old NHS by strategic authorities such as
DHAs and RHAs. This is, however, only the minimum interpretation of
what a shift from need to demand is likely to entail. It could be reinforced
by top-up payments.

A VOUCHER SYSTEM?

It is but a small step from creation of an internal market which is purchaser-driven to institution of a system in which top-up payments are
sanctioned. At this point, the NHS would approach a voucher system, in
which all citizens were provided with a voucher to cover the cost of basic
NHS services, and were required to fund for themselves any provision
above this basic level.

This may be both in line with the basic tenets of a market system and the
only feasible way of increasing overall health spending in future years
(which are likely to be as tax-resistant as is the present age). In no
sense, however, is it consonant with the basic distributive principles on
which the NHS was founded. Notions of social justice could therefore be
a major casualty of the NHS reforms as need is superseded by
demand.

It must be stressed that the possibility of such a development is strongly
rejected by government ministers, and is certainly not to be expected in
the foreseeable future. As a logical extension of the internal market programme it is not, however, to be ruled out as a more distant prospect.

CHOICE VERSUS SOCIAL JUSTICE

As with all political change, the perceived desirability of health reform
depends on values placed on the various factors which are being traded
off by it. Here, the equation is fairly straightforward and, indeed,
familiar: increased choice and autonomy for decreased equality and
social justice.

Under any conditions, judging between these competing values is extremely difficult. It might be noted that the government has a reserve argument to deploy against those whose judgment conflicts with its own. This consists in the claim that increased efficiency generated by a quasi-market solution in health will produce gains for all. In this way, it claims, everyone will benefit from the reform programme (even if some will benefit more than others). Here, then, the standard Conservative conviction that efficiency is produced by competition rather than by attempts at strategic planning is in evidence. It is by no means uncontestable, though the decisive evidence against planning on the really grand scale which has been amassed in post-war years is increasingly being supplemented by evidence which suggests that even lesser scale planning may be less efficient than is claimed by its protagonists.

Assessments of the justice of Britain's health care arrangements will be affected in two main ways by the fragmentation and increased diversity generated by the internal market reforms. On the one hand, the range of British health care outcomes will almost certainly be increased by the new diversity of provision in the primary care sector. Yet on the other the health care needs of disadvantaged sections of the British population could be met in improved ways by incentives to register such people written into the 1990 GPs' – and dentists' – contracts. Here, then, the balance of judgment is equivocal. Some might endorse the improved position of the least well-off in society. A strict egalitarian would, however, object to increased diversity in health care outcomes.

In a more general sense, the precise way in which the equation of choice and social justice is interpreted is problematic. For most people it must depend on the magnitudes involved on each side of the equation. These cannot yet be measured with any accuracy.

THE NEW NHS ASSESSED

Assessment of strengths and weaknesses of the new NHS does not produce a clear reckoning. The shift in emphasis from secondary to primary care is certainly welcome, for hospitals have long been major and often inefficient consumers of NHS resources. The associated promotion of preventive medicine is also a positive step.

Beyond this, integration of the entire health care system could be enhanced by the internal market reforms. Indeed, GPs' purchasing function could conceivably stretch across the entire spectrum of care, thereby generating the kind of integration between different branches of Britain's health care system which has long been sought, but never actually secured. The possibility of this happening is, too, a benefit.

Yet there are also clear weaknesses in the reform programme. Some are probably no more than short term. Competition remains minimal, and the information systems on which it is based are still only developing. Each of these problems is likely to be largely overcome in due course. More important are structural defects of the new NHS. Chief among these is the extreme fragmentation – and thus potentially extreme diversity of provision – generated by GP fundholding.

In short, the old NHS commitment to provision of universal health coverage on the basis not of income or advantage, but simply of need, is substantially threatened by the fragmentation which Bevan saw in the Beveridge plan, and did all he could to avoid. Limitations of the marketised NHS as currently conceived thus leave clear room for consideration of alternative health care futures. Three areas of funding, delivery and access are considered in the chapters which follow.

8 HEALTH CARE FUNDING

The central issue which the NHS Review was established in 1988 to investigate, but which it in fact decided to make no fundamental alteration to, was the NHS funding regime. Policy makers' continuing conservatism in this regard means that the new NHS, like the old, is financed mainly out of general taxation. This does not necessarily mean, however, that the present NHS funding regime is the best that could be devised.

THE PRESENT SITUATION

Despite substantial increases in health fees and charges during the 1980s, and a proliferation of income-raising schemes and initiatives in hospitals up and down the country, the NHS remains predominantly tax-funded. A mere 4 per cent of NHS finance currently comes from fees and charges combined. It is true that 4 per cent of £34.4 billion is a lot of money – nearly £1.4 billion – and that it enables all sorts of treatments to be provided which would otherwise be impossible. Nevertheless, it remains the case that the NHS continues to be almost wholly financed out of the national exchequer.

Because even Margaret Thatcher's fundamental review failed to come up with an alternative to historic means of funding the NHS, that arrangement has developed a greater aura of permanence than almost any other aspect of the British health care system, and justifiably so. It remains one of the few aspects of the NHS around which politicians of all parties claim to unite.

Yet at the same time the British public continually demonstrates substantial dissatisfaction with NHS funding arrangements, believing not so much that the basic system of tax funding is mistaken or in some sense unjust, but that the NHS should not be starved of cash on such a regular – indeed permanent – basis. Underfunding continues to be a central allegation laid at the door of NHS policy makers.

The rise in health insurance registrations in the 1980s – which must at least in part indicate dissatisfaction with the NHS – has already been noted. For the vast majority of British people, however, exit from state-funded health provision is not now, and is unlikely in the foreseeable future to become, a realistic option. In circumstances when people's loyalty is stretched to – and indeed beyond – the limit, their only feasible option is therefore to voice their complaints.

This people have done increasingly in recent years with respect to welfare services in general and to health services in particular. Public concern about the (low) level of NHS funding is demonstrated very clearly by *British Social Attitudes* opinion surveys. Throughout the 1980s, health consistently topped the list of services on which people would like to see increased public spending, registering its proportion of favourable responses at 35 per cent in 1985 and at 38 per cent in 1990.

Yet there is of course a paradox here, for just as support for increased welfare spending has risen consistently since the late 1970s, so the British people have equally consistently returned the very Conservative governments which have been held (whether justifiably or not) uniquely responsible for underfunding of the NHS and other welfare services over that same period. The most evident case of this was the 1992 general election, when an apparently electable Labour Party – which had done all it could to raise the profile of health issues both before and during the election campaign – was in the end well beaten by a Conservative Party which was held to be notably weak on health and other social issues. The British people, it seemed, were very keen on extra health spending so long as their own personal tax burden did not thereby increase.

In these circumstances, health care funding requires investigation. Is the NHS doomed by tax-resistant voters to permanent cash crisis? Or could a new set of funding arrangements be devised which would release it from the trap in which it is currently caught? An entire series of answers can be given to these linked questions, for many different means of funding health care are conceivable. If peripheral funding options – such as fees and charges – are disregarded, four core funding options remain.

DIRECT STATE FUNDING OUT OF GENERAL TAXATION

Direct state funding out of general taxation is currently the central mechanism employed in the UK to fund health care. This is, then, the baseline against which all other funding options must be judged.

Its advantages are many. It is cheap, in that the Treasury usually exercises tight control over the global health budget and at the very least ensures that health expenditure never spirals completely out of control (as has come close to happening in some other countries, notably the USA). It is also administratively inexpensive, in that funding is simply transferred from central government to lower tiers in the NHS hierarchy. In addition it is relatively flexible, in that marginal increases in the health budget can be made reasonably easily, either by a slight reordering of government priorities, or by withdrawing funds from the Treasury's Contingency Reserve, or, if absolutely necessary, by a slight increase in general taxation. Furthermore, it is predictable in its yield, in that government can usually be relied on to deliver the health care funding which has been agreed in the annual spending round. Finally, direct state funding out of general taxation is also socially just in the eyes of many.

Compared with this long list of advantages, the disadvantages of direct state funding out of general taxation might seem slight and, indeed, unimportant. The chief disadvantages are twofold. The first is that direct state funding is unresponsive to social demands for increases in public spending on health. Governments inevitably view health spending as part of their wider programme of economic management, and are reluctant to accede to demands for increased funding when those demands conflict with their more general economic strategy. Secondly, direct state funding is seen by some as limiting the sphere of individual choice in health provision.

This may be only a very small list of disadvantages, but it should not be dismissed as unimportant. In recent years the NHS has been criticised on both counts listed here, particularly the first.

A HEALTH TAX

Two main ways of tackling this first and in recent years highly important disadvantage have been proposed. To begin with, the idea of direct state funding by means of a health tax has been suggested.

This proposal shares many features – and advantages – with existing financing arrangements. However, if a health tax were implemented, health funding would no longer come out of the general pool of taxes collected each year by the state. Instead, it would be ring-fenced or, in technical terms, hypothecated. That is to say that the health tax would not only be clearly identified in national accounts, but would also appear as a separate line entry on individuals' tax demands and statements. It could, of course, be either flat-rate or graduated.

The main advantage of a health tax is that it might help to solve the paradox of the Thatcher and post-Thatcher years, that people consistently vote for increased health spending in opinion polls and against it in real polls at general elections. If a hypothecated health tax were introduced governments would be able to tap the deep reservoir of public support which the NHS undoubtedly commands – and increase health taxes – without compromising their general line on taxation which, in the current climate, cannot afford to be based on anything other than a philosophy of retrenchment. Furthermore, a health tax would make it very easy to hold governments to account on their health record, for election promises with regard to health spending would be immediately testable against a highly visible health tax.

The central advantage of this proposal is, then, that it could succeed in transferring power from governments to individuals by significantly increasing the public's ability to express a clear preference with regard to health spending. Indeed, it is even possible to take the proposal a stage further, and argue that the exact rate at which a health tax is set should be determined by direct vote on an annual basis. If the idea of an annual health referendum were adopted, health funding would be released from many of the constraints of normal party political debate, and governments would simply be mandated by direct popular vote to set a given level of taxation and thereby generate a reasonably predictable level of health spending. Health would then be under significantly greater popular control than is the case at present.

This extension of health care democracy is not, however, without problems. Chief among them is that of control. Under the present system, very clear control over global health care spending is exercised by the Treasury. Were the level of health spending to be set not by elected politicians, but instead by annual expressions of the popular will elicited through referenda, this central control mechanism would be undermined. The Treasury would become no more than a lone participant in a very open national debate. The substantial power which it exercises through the annual spending round would be significantly cut. In these circumstances, health care spending might spiral out of control, particularly if debate became dominated by the medical profession and its constant calls for extra funding.

Yet to make this objection is to express doubts about the viability and validity of democracy itself, and also to suggest that the public's present and probable future resistance to taxation in general would have no purchase in the health sphere. This seems highly unlikely. Far more likely is that health would be debated in a more informed manner than is the case at present, with the likely costs of any given proposal being as visible to the general public as expected benefits. This is very much not the case under our present arrangements, which largely obscure the funding implications of increases in health spending by enveloping them in the general – and very large – category of annual public expenditure. Only alleged benefits of extra spending have a high profile in public debate. A hypothecated health tax would contribute to that debate, and would thereby represent an extension of British democracy.

Two problems remain. One is essentially practical and political. It has been raised by the current NHS Chief Executive, Duncan Nichol. Nichol argues that hypothecation is not feasible because no government with economic management responsibilities can be expected to allow such a large element of public spending to slip from its control. This is certainly a valid point, for all governments are strongly protective of all powers which they currently possess. However, it is in no sense strong enough to undermine the argument in favour of hypothecation. Were public debate and the democratic process to be extended by means of a hypothecated health tax, governments would simply have to convince the general public of the merits of their case for restrictions on health spending, rather than retaining reserve powers (as they do currently) to impose their will even when they have lost the debate. Furthermore, as has already been argued, there is no reason to assume that the public would immediately lose all fiscal caution when faced with a health tax.

The second remaining problem is essentially practical and fiscal. It is that the health care funding would become too buoyant, rising in economic booms and falling in slumps as the health tax responded to overall changes in the tax take. This may be welcome in a boom, but could herald disaster in a slump. Yet even this problem is not insurmountable. In conditions of slump, when health tax revenues are likely to fall, it would be incumbent on government to make a case for increasing the (health) tax burden. Only continuing popularity would provide the NHS with sure defences.

A health tax is therefore a powerful alternative to current arrangements. It offers a funding mechanism which is a good deal more responsive and democratic than is the present funding system.

SOCIAL INSURANCE

Similar advantages could be generated by means of the second main way of overcoming the central disadvantage associated with Britain's current arrangements for funding public health care, that they are unresponsive to social demands for increases in health spending. This is a social insurance scheme, which, like hypothecation, is a way of earmarking funds for health care provision.

In essence, social insurance is compulsory individual insurance. Instead of collecting taxes from individuals and passing them on to health care agencies, government obliges individuals to take out health insurance cover for themselves. The two processes look different but are in some ways similar, particularly if on the one hand the taxation mode involves hypothecation, and on the other the social insurance mode involves central collection of funds. In each case individuals have no choice but to pay for health cover, for social insurance schemes (like taxation regimes) have universal membership. Furthermore, just as taxation can be progressive, regressive or neutral in its impacts, so too can social insurance. If it so chooses, government can easily build redistributive objectives into the rules it lays down for social insurance. Social insurance is the predominant mode of health funding in continental Europe.

However, it is important to stress one major difference between taxation and real social insurance. This is that a health service which is funded out of general taxation extends health care to all on the basis of citizenship, and takes no account of individual tax payments. A social insurance scheme, by contrast, undercuts the general citizenship qualification by introducing on the one hand a relation between payments into the insurance fund and health care entitlements, and on the other an actuarial calculation of risk. One consequence may be seen to strike at the heart of contemporary notions of citizenship, the other to generate high premiums for groups which are least likely to be able to afford them. For these two reasons, proper insurance principles never apply in practice. As a core funding regime, social insurance is therefore undesirable.

PRIVATE INSURANCE

An alternative to the compulsory regime of social insurance is private insurance. In the United States this is the main health care funding mechanism, although publicly-funded schemes also exist. Only rarely is it strictly voluntary. For most Americans who have it, it is a condition of employment.

Perhaps the most fundamental problem associated with private insurance is moral. Despite the rhetoric of choice and freedom which has been heard increasingly in Britain in recent years, we retain a commitment as a civilised society to certain basic, universal standards of health care. Put another way, we are unwilling to allow anyone to make the possibly catastrophic choice of having no health cover whatsoever. To this extent, we remain committed to the paternalistic state, which directs us to our own best interests by forcing us to take out health care cover.

Indeed, even the United States, one of the most individualistic societies in the world, has developed federal programmes designed to protect all members of society from catastrophic health outcomes. Part of Lyndon Johnson's Great Society initiative, the twin federal programmes Medicare (which provides basic state-funded coverage for old people) and Medicaid (which provides similar coverage for the poor) were established in the mid-1960s to offer safety-net health care provision to all Americans. In neither case has this happened.

However, the fact that these two programmes actually fail to offer even safety-net health care provision to 35 million Americans who have no health cover whatsoever, and whose health needs are met (if at all) on often ad hoc bases at the local level, is an indictment of American political practice. It does not demolish the central argument advanced here, that no civilised society will allow its citizens complete freedom of choice in providing for their health care needs.

Private insurance presents a further problem. This is cost explosion. In America there is a direct link between the predominant mode of health care funding and chronic cost increases. Costs in the American health care system have spiralled at least in part because of the private insurance basis on which it predominantly functions. The explanation for this linkage is the perverse set of incentives which is built into the system.

At the centre of this perverse set is an incentive to treat. In the American private health care sector, doctors have a strong incentive to treat because they are remunerated not on a fixed or per capita basis, but strictly on the variable basis of direct payment for services and treatments rendered. The more they treat, the more they are able to bill insurance companies, and the more they receive in payment. Americans, partly in consequence (though partly one suspects for other, cultural, reasons), are the most cared-for nation on earth. At the same time, of course, access to care for some Americans is as bad as anywhere in the industrialised world.

The cost problem in the American private health sector might be controllable were there an effective forum in which the global outcome of individual treatment decisions were discussed. If, for example, health care costs were aggregated and debated as they are in European political systems, then some kind of controlling pressure from above might be established. This, however, does not happen, and such initiatives as there have been have had to operate at a more decentralised level.

The relevance of American experience to the wider debate about possible NHS funding futures is that it indicates the difficulties associated with private health insurance. These stretch from moral objections to the very great practical problem of cost explosion. Whilst some of these problems can be overcome in part, the fundamental flaw would seem to be systemic. Voluntary insurance is simply the wrong solution to core health care funding, no matter how great its virtues in terms of individual freedom.

HEALTH CARE FUNDING SCHEMES ASSESSED

Only financing arrangements based on some form of taxation offer acceptable means of core funding a national health care system. Both general taxation and a health tax have associated advantages and disadvantages. On grounds of popular control, a case may be made for a health tax.

However, debate need not stop here. It may be that the best regime is generated by combining more than one system of health care funding. Indeed, by levying a health tax on all, basic citizenship criteria may be met. By allowing individuals to opt out of a health tax on condition that they take out health insurance to at least an equivalent value, responsiveness and choice criteria may be met. Although ring-fenced health taxes are rare, the possibility of opt out is, in fact, not unlike arrangements which currently exist in some European countries. Both Germany and Holland allow individuals to opt out of tax-funded health provision and into a form of social insurance.

Provisions for opting out of a health tax in order to take out health insurance may sound rather similar to existing British arrangements. There is, however, a key difference. The proposal advanced here is that individuals who choose to opt out of tax-funded health care should have their contribution reimbursed in order that they may spend it on health insurance. Under current British arrangements, people who take out health insurance pay twice for health care. On libertarian grounds, an alteration to this arrangement is desirable.

Beyond this, provision for top-up payments could be increased. Individual payments will never constitute an acceptable core funding option for the NHS. However, as a peripheral funding option they could be encouraged both on grounds of choice and freedom, and as a means of increasing the total amount of resources available to the NHS. The two-tier system which would inevitably result would differ only in degree, not kind, from existing arrangements. In a free society, diversity in health care outcomes is unavoidable. In the health care sphere, as in others, limits on individual purchasing decisions can never be total.

NEW FUNDING ARRANGEMENTS FOR THE NHS

The answer to the key question posed at the start of this chapter is therefore that the NHS need not be doomed by tax-resistant (but pro-NHS) voters to permanent cash crisis. A new set of core funding arrangements could certainly be devised which would release it from the trap in which it is currently caught. Peripheral funding could also be increased, but by definition it will never be sufficient to meet the main needs of the health care sector. A composite health tax and social insurance scheme offers the best NHS funding future.

If such a scheme is deemed desirable, the final matter which needs to be considered is means by which a shift in NHS funding arrangements could be made. The obvious way forward is to embark on a two-stage reform process. First, health care funding could be stripped out of general taxation and hypothecated. Secondly, a health tax could have a social insurance component grafted on to it. Initially any such scheme would need to conform quite closely to the tax structure it was replacing. Over time, however, it could take on its own character.

9 HEALTH CARE DELIVERY

The NHS Review, set up in 1988 to investigate alternative modes of funding core health services in Britain, turned out to be entirely conservative in its funding recommendations. It chose instead to focus its reforming energies on health care delivery, and to outline extensive changes to the way in which UK health services are organised and managed. The result was fragmentation and marketisation of the NHS, which seem likely to generate many gains, but also quite possibly extensive losses.

BACK TO STRATEGIC PLANNING?

One alternative to the present reform programme would seem to be to return to strategic planning. However, it is important to state at the outset that this option does not in fact exist. It is the system by which the old NHS, at least by the end, was intended to operate. Yet in reality it never lived up to this ideal, and was never likely to. In itself, this is powerful commentary on the feasibility and desirability of this type of arrangement.

Behind the facade of a planned and virtuous NHS, the reality was rather different. The old NHS had a number of disadvantages, central among them being the fact that even with the introduction of general management it remained in many ways a professionally-run service. Such an arrangement was bound to come under attack as politicians sought greater control over outcomes and as the general public began to abandon its traditional trust in professional judgments. Perhaps most importantly, however, the central principle of medical autonomy was a major obstacle to all attempts at health service planning. In consequence, the old NHS was highly cumbersome and inflexible.

It also contained odd incentive structures, such that by the 1980s all sorts of perverse incentives were coming to light. Block funding of hospitals, for example, operated to reward those hospitals which treated less patients and to penalise those which treated more. Similarly, consultants in hospitals had no clear incentive to improve their service to patients, although many of them nevertheless sought to do so. On top of this, there was little possibility of change being driven from the base of the service through consumer demand. The old NHS was centred on large general hospitals, which were in many ways immune to change even though they were becoming increasingly out-moded as the 1980s wore on.

It is important to note that these disadvantages were not readily remediable within the old NHS structure. General management had some impact on consultants' medical decision making, and the introduction of new information systems at least opened up the possibility of professional accountability. Change within the confines of the old system did not, however, promise revolutionary alterations as they did not do enough to tackle the fundamental problem, which was professional autonomy itself.

A BETTER FORM OF MARKETISATION?

The mechanism which is currently being employed to undermine professional autonomy – in the name of choice, efficiency, responsiveness and a series of lesser values – is marketisation. Just as the spread of capitalism dissolved many feudal hierarchies (in the process replacing them with new ones of its own), so development of the NHS internal market is being used to break down existing medical hierarchies.

Yet the way in which marketisation is being pursued in the NHS is by fragmentation of demand through creation of GP fundholders. It is from this fragmentation that many undesirable features of the new NHS emanate. These features need not, however, be generated by marketisation. Indeed, if marketisation can be dissociated from fragmentation, then a series of advantages can be secured by it. Marketisation not only allows the price mechanism to operate as an efficient signalling system within the health care sector, but also imposes a crucial discipline on medical behaviour. No longer are professionals protected from market forces by a self-contained and monolithic planned system.

It also has disadvantages, which relate chiefly to diverse, unequal and undesirable outcomes. Whilst market incentives may be entirely acceptable in other spheres, in health they are themselves likely to be perverse. At base, the problem is that the profit motive is not an entirely satisfactory determinant of medical behaviour, for the bottom line in health care is not profit, but health.

The task, then, is twofold. First, it is to determine whether the advantages of marketisation can be secured without fragmentation. Secondly, it is to determine means by which the inherent disadvantages of marketisation itself can be overcome by a health care system. The present reform programme does not manage these tasks as well as it might.

BACK TO ENTHOVEN

In considering how a better form of marketisation might be generated, it is useful to reconsider the proposal made byEnthoven which triggered the entire internal market reform process. This made the key purchaser-provider distinction which lies at the heart of the internal market. However, on the crucial purchaser side of that market it instituted not GP fundholders, but something much closer to the health maintenance organisations that have been (gradually) developed in America during the past 20 years. These are health care purchasing agencies, with minimum list sizes of 50 000 patients, which buy both primary and secondary care on behalf of their registered patients. They may or may not employ their own salaried doctors and consultants. HMOs do not need to be specific to a particular locality, but can operate on a nationwide (or even cross-national) scale. Businesses, trade unions or voluntary associations are the kinds of institution through which they might emerge.

The most evident difference between Enthoven's HMOs and GP fundholders is the difference in their list sizes. Immediately, Enthoven's plan substantially reduces the extent of fragmentation caused by GP fundholding, and helps to overcome the problem that fundholding practices operate on too small a scale to bear the full scale of patient risk. Abolition, or at least substantial reduction of the extent, of provisions to cover this problem would be possible under his system. In the primary care sector of the NHS, such action is not feasible when the purchasing unit is too small to meet the cost of catastrophic cover. In a regime of GP fundholders, the only possible way out is to encourage fundholding practices to combine as a means of spreading risk. In effect, they would thereby reconstitute themselves on the Enthoven model.

There are, however, further advantages in the Enthoven plan. It generates more individual choice than GP fundholding, for constraints of geography and information deficits can be reduced by it. Indeed, HMOs (like other insurance organisations) need have no geographical limitations. Furthermore, the fact that they will therefore operate in genuine competition with each other is likely to increase the amount of information available to individuals. Most importantly, the Enthoven plan substantially reduces fragmentation in the internal market, which suggests that diversity of health care outcomes would be reduced. In place of literally thousands of fundholding practices, Enthoven would institute a relatively small number of HMOs – perhaps several hundred – which could be monitored and regulated in ways which will not be possible if and when all general practices have become fundholding.

The Enthoven plan thereby makes significant advances on GP fundholding. It is, nevertheless, vulnerable to more intractable problems of a market for health care. These can only be overcome by means of specific regulations and controls.

SKIMMING

One very basic problem is skimming. In a health care system this is the process whereby individuals and institutions which are block funded for treatments seek to attract healthy patients who are likely to impose only small costs on their funds, and to off-load on to others sick patients who are likely to impose high costs. It is not difficult to see that undesirable outcomes are likely to result from such practices.

In the new NHS, this problem relates particularly to GP fundholding, where it has the potential to become substantial. This is because a large part of GP fundholder budgets is derived from capitation fees and is thus likely to generate skimming problems. It looms equally large in the case of HMOs. On the provider side of the internal market it is less substantial, because secondary care units are partially funded in direct relation to services rendered.

The problem of skimming by GP fundholders can be addressed in two ways. On the one hand, open registration can be partnered by right of registration, such that patients have a right to register with the GP or practice of their choice, and GPs themselves have much less scope for indulging in skimming. On the other, capitation fees can be weighted according to various 'objective' criteria, such as age, family medical history, occupation, region, and so on, so that the extent of bad risks is reduced.

Both devices feature in some form in the new NHS, and each could easily be applied to reform on the Enthoven model. Neither is infallible, but each serves to reduce the skimming problem to a considerable extent.

SKIMPING

A second cause for concern in a marketised health care system is skimping. This is the process whereby purchasers and providers in a health market seek to reduce their costs by skimping on the treatment they give patients. This difficulty is again particularly pressing on the purchaser side of the internal market.

To the extent that real competition is generated by the internal market, providers are likely to be disciplined by purchaser pressure. Purchasers themselves are less readily held to account. This is because individuals – who might exercise a controlling function – have very little expertise in assessing medical performance. For this reason, skimping presents particular problems on the purchaser side of a health care market. In other markets, the problem is diminished, because the purchaser is also the consumer of goods and services which are purchased. In a market in which individuals cede purchasing power to another agent, and in which they themselves are in any case never likely to possess sufficient information to make an independent assessment of their own best interests, the problem becomes real.

The central attribute of a market system – that it generates competition for custom – may therefore operate in health care as elsewhere to prevent adverse outcomes arising from skimping. A purchasing agency which gains a reputation for skimping will soon lose custom, such that some short-term problems should be overcome in the long-term. Yet, for two reasons, this is not an entirely satisfactory resolution of the problem. To begin with, skimping pressures may well be global in the new NHS. Indeed, competition could easily operate to increase such pressures, for in seeking to meet the challenges of competition GP fundholders may actually find themselves obliged to cut corners. Secondly, skimping is likely to be disproportionately harmful to poor, disadvantaged and inarticulate sections of the population, and thereby raises the spectre of increased inequality of core health care distribution in the new NHS.

In the NHS internal market, only formal regulation procedures – embodied in medical audit and, perhaps, a charter of patients' rights – can ensure that skimping does not become a substantial problem. Similar procedures would have to be applied to reform along the lines recommended by Enthoven.

NEW DELIVERY ARRANGEMENTS FOR THE NHS

A marketised system has clear advantages in terms of choice, efficiency and responsiveness. However, it is not necessary to go to the extreme of extensive system fragmentation to secure all of these.

The efficiency gains which have been widely advertised as desirable properties of markets do not, for example, require the institution of GP fundholders. They can equally be secured by means of the Enthoven proposal. Furthermore, a substantial element of choice can be written into the Enthoven plan by allowing individuals to contract health care delivery from any one of the many health maintenance organisations operating in his internal market. Responsiveness is likely to be greater in a system of HMOs than in a system of GP fundholders.

On each of these counts, a central aspect of the NHS reforms seems fundamentally misguided. GP fundholding poses a very substantial threat to many of the basic principles on which the NHS was founded. Moreover, it does so for no very good reason. Many of the benefits which fundholding is said to bring with it are actually generated merely by the purchaser-provider distinction, which does not require GP fundholding.

On this basis, it is possible to argue that the NHS reforms, far from making an important step forward in the evolution of the Service, will in fact operate to undermine many of its fundamental principles. The new NHS will be a far less satisfactory creation than it could, and should, be. Whilst many benefits may flow from the reform programme, the founding principle of provision of core health care services according only to criteria of need may be fatally compromised.

This aspect of the NHS reforms provokes genuine concern. As was argued in Chapter 8, it is acceptable to allow individuals to purchase additional or premium health care. Core health servics should not, however, be distributed on a fundamentally differential basis. Yet this is the prospect that GP fundholding presents. Far more satisfactory than GP fundholding would be a system based on the Enthoven model of HMOs. It would not necessarily – indeed, it would certainly not – secure full equality of health care outcomes. It would, however, be far more easy to regulate than is a system of GP fundholders, and might even perform by egalitarian measures on a par with the old NHS.

10 ACCESS TO HEALTH CARE

Consideration of alternative mechanisms of health care delivery leads inevitably to debate of access to health care. In the old NHS, this was neither equal nor particularly open. However, few people seemed to bother about – or even notice – these aspects of the old system. In the new NHS, access is likely to become a far more contentious issue. This is partly because the mechanisms of the new NHS make problems and inequalities in access far more visible, partly because people are in any case demanding more say over the health care they receive, and partly because the government has taken up the issue of access in its *Patient's Charter*.

THE PROBLEM OF ACCESS

It is sometimes argued that the problem of access to health care within the NHS would disappear if only sufficient resources were provided. Yet virtually infinite amounts could be spent on health care if all demands were simply met by a financially-unrestricted NHS. At some point, a limit must be placed on demand.

At this point, the issue of rationing has to be addressed. If some demands for health care are to be denied, then rationing criteria must be developed, even if it is only in an informal or hidden sense. Indeed, it was in just this manner that rationing was managed by the old NHS. Behind the veil of 'professional judgment' and 'medical opinion', a great deal of rationing was undertaken for strictly financial reasons, and was no less proper for that.

This system is, however, breaking down with the shift to a more open and accountable NHS. In these circumstances, the old paternalist criteria by which access used to be determined in the NHS are in need of replacement. The system which will take their place is not yet properly evident.

RATIONING: A MARKET SOLUTION?

On one reading of the internal market reforms, rationing will be determined by market criteria in the new NHS as GP fundholders

shop around for patient treatment. However, even the extent of fragmentation generated by GP fundholding will not take the NHS all the
way to this extreme. The internal market will certainly remain regulated
and at least partially directed for the foreseeable future.

It is in fact highly desirable that this should be so, for few would consider a market solution to health care distribution to be just. Indeed, it is
precisely at this point that the internal market reforms have been criticised
here. Their major failing is that they undermine regulated health care provision to an excessive extent, and generate undesirable distributions.

If, then, an argument for strategic assessment of health needs is to be sustained, the criteria by which judgments concerning rationing are to be
developed require specification.

RATIONING: A 'SCIENTIFIC' SOLUTION

It might be thought that one way of establishing rationing criteria is by
scientific means. Indeed, health care professionals are already starting to
float the idea of measuring the value of competing treatments by
quality-adjusted life years (QALYs), and similar yardsticks.

The intention is to generate rationing criteria by means of cost-benefit
analysis. Costs of different treatments are now emerging through the pricing information generated by the new NHS. Benefits could be
assessed by means of QALYs. There are, however, several problems
with such an approach. To begin with, QALYs are not particularly scientific, but in fact contain a large subjective component (relating to
definitions of 'quality'). In addition, it is not clear that even a perfect QALY
index would in fact measure the sorts of things that should be
accounted for in setting rationing criteria. Certain treatments may
rank some distance from the top of a QALY index, but still be deemed
desirable by a given society. Treatment for kidney failure is, for example,
expensive and often generates a low ranking on QALY indices. Yet
public endorsement of any attempt substantially to restrict provision of
it is likely to be very limited.

QALYs may be helpful in contributing to rationing debates, but they
could never in themselves resolve all the dilemmas of health policy
which confront any society. In the end, such dilemmas can only be
resolved by political means.

RATIONING: THE OREGON SOLUTION

Explicit political debate of rationing remains extremely limited. In one American state, however, a serious attempt has been made to develop a series of formal rationing criteria by political means. The Oregon solution is therefore worth investigating in some detail.[1]

The beginnings of a new approach to health care rationing were developed in Oregon in an attempt to address head-on the tension between unlimited demand for health care and finite resources. By the late 1980s this eternal problem had generated a situation in Oregon in which only those with incomes at 58 per cent or less of the federal poverty level qualified for state-funded treatment through Medicaid. Many anomalies resulted. Partly in consequence, state politicians passed a package of laws (centred on the Oregon Basic Health Services Act, legislated in July 1989) which set in motion a process of explicit rationing.

This package of laws invited the public to join in drawing up a list of priority health treatments, ranked in the order in which they should be made available through the state health programme. A Health Services Commission was appointed to oversee the task of constructing this list. It sponsored or itself conducted more than 50 community meetings across the state, and a random telephone survey of 1000 people.

The extent of public participation in the Oregon scheme should not be exaggerated. Dominance of the Health Services Commission by health care professionals allowed doctors a disproportionate say in drawing up the rank listing. However, they may have gained this pre-eminent position as much by default as by anything else. In truth, the Oregon public showed little interest in the prioritisation exercise, as is perhaps indicated by the very limited coverage it received in the single state-wide paper, the *Oregonian*. Public participation could undoubtedly have been greater had it been sought by the Oregon public.

Initial listings revealed some 'odd' priorities: crooked teeth ranked higher than early treatment for Hodgkin's disease, reconstructive breast surgery ranked higher than treatment for open fracture of the thigh, and treatment for thumb-sucking ranked higher than hospitalisation of a child for starvation. Treatment for AIDS received a very low ranking.[2] Yet it would be difficult to argue that these 'oddities' are not genuinely expressive of widely-held American values. The most glaring ones were nevertheless excised by health care professionals on the Health Services Commission.

The eventual result was a rank listing of 709 possible health care treatments or services, released in February 1991. The next operation was straight forward. By matching available state funds against the costed list of prioritised services, the extent of possible provision was revealed. It turned out that only the top 587 treatments could be funded from existing funding allocations. All treatments from rank order 588 to 709 were therefore struck off the publicly-funded list of health care treatments.

RATIONING: OREGON CONSIDERED

This appears to be – and indeed is – a rather brutal means of allocating health resources. However, it is in some ways more open, accountable and, therefore (it might be argued) fair than the system which operated in the old NHS, and will continue to operate to some extent in the new. Instead of decisions of life and death being taken behind the veil of medical opinion, they are apparently brought into the open and made collectively. Definition of an adequate minimum standard of health care becomes, it would seem, a public process.

Yet the extent to which medical opinion was undermined in Oregon can be exaggerated. Key decisions on prioritisation were made not by the public in open fora, but by medical professionals who refined crude public orderings into the final rank listing. Participatory debate was in many ways undermined by medical judgment. This is, perhaps, inevitable in an area in which no judgment is straight forward and some element of expert opinion must necessarily be exercised. It is also in part a product of widespread apathy among Oregonians. The fundamental problem is however that no rationing formula could ever be devised, for the entire question of health care prioritisation is simply too complex to permit use of mechanical indices of distribution.[3]

Nevertheless, the Oregon solution should not simply be dismissed as just another means of allowing medical opinion to dictate to the public. The increase in health care information which it affords, and the detailed listing of services which can or (more importantly) cannot be financed, must do something to concentrate people's minds and must thereby enable debate to take place on a more informed and precise basis than is usually the case. In a sense, health care consciousness is raised by open debate of rationing.

The Oregon solution is not therefore to be criticised for alleged brutality. It scores no more highly by this measure than many other health systems, and is in some ways more just than are they. It in no sense provides the solution to rationing, but its involvement of the public in some form of health debate must be both welcome and at least some kind of check on medical judgment.

HEALTH TARGETS

Rationing of health care will never be conducted in an entirely satisfactory manner. One way of informing debate about prioritisation and rationing is development of health targets. These relate not to health care, but to health outcomes. Their use is that they can be publicly agreed and then allowed to feed into decisions concerning the sorts of treatment which should be made available by a public health care system. In essence, the public agrees health targets and permits medical judgment to determine means by which they are best attained.

This is, then, a way of improving on the kind of exercise which was conducted in Oregon. It is highly necessary, for any society which takes upon itself a public health responsibility also needs to develop a public health strategy. This should set attainable targets. Moreover, it should be framed within the broad set of ideals to which the society is committed, respecting individual choice as currently understood as an important prerequisite. The argument that health gains will result from a particular prohibition or injunction is both necessary and yet not sufficient to ensure its adoption.

One benefit of creation of the purchaser-provider distinction in health is that it makes development of a public health strategy more feasible by divorcing strategic institutions from involvement in the minutiae of provision. This does not mean that RHAs and DHAs will immediately become the people's champions which William Waldegrave in a flight of rhetoric thought they might become.[4] At least under present arrangements, they will remain aware of the limits on funding required to meet the cost of any targets which might be agreed. Nevertheless, the basic separation of roles is at least helpful in this regard.

It has in fact been accompanied by elaboration of Britain's first set of public health targets. For England, these are contained in the White Paper, *The Health of the Nation*, published by Health Secretary Virginia Bottomley in July 1992 (following publication of a draft by Waldegrave in June 1991). This was the first explicit move in this direction on the part of the Department of Health. It means that all four constituent nations of the UK have now started to set health targets, partly as a response to the World Health Organisation's (WHO) 'Health for All 2000' initiative launched at the end of the 1970s. Although they might never become 'champions of the people', health authorities can nevertheless be expected to encourage GPs to use their purchasing power to meet the targets which have been set and agreed nationally.

Included in five key areas identified by the White Paper are the following target reductions:
- Death from coronary heart disease and stroke: 40 per cent by the year 2000
- Death from breast cancer: 25 per cent by 2000
- Death from lung cancer: 30 per cent in men and 15 per cent in women by 2010
- Suicide: 15 per cent by 2000
- Conception among under-16s: 50 per cent by 2000
- Gonorrhoea (because of its relation to AIDS trends): 20 per cent by 1995.
- Accidental deaths: 33 per cent among under-15s and 25 per cent among people aged 15-25 by 2005

Progress towards these targets will be monitored by a ministerial cabinet committee covering 11 government departments, which will also take soundings from local authorities, voluntary organisations, the media and employers.

Attainment of some of these targets depends on factors well outside the traditional province of the Department of Health. Suicide, teenage pregnancy and accidental deaths have very strong cultural components, and are not in any strict sense health-related. Yet the exercise is still welcome for its contribution to public health strategy. Whilst it is possible to argue over details, it is difficult to maintain that an approach of this kind is itself at fault. At the very least, it is a step in the right direction.

PUBLIC HEALTH

Beyond this, it is necessary for public policy to take a more coordinated view of health futures. Again there are trade-offs to be made, but a government which assumes formal responsibility for the health of the nation needs to develop a strategic approach to health policy.

This is not to argue that health is not a private responsibility – undoubtedly it is – but to maintain that something akin to the public health movement of the Victorian years needs to be regenerated. This would involve governments in elaborating a much clearer health policy line than has been the case in recent years. Indeed, the twin and much-criticised failures of *The Health of the Nation* to take a stance on tobacco advertising or even to address the relation between poverty and poor health may properly be questioned in this context.

Nevertheless, since publication in January 1988 of the Acheson Report on public health, it has been clear that British public policy is moving in the direction of a more developed public health stance. This report was in fact the first government-sponsored review of the public health function in Britain since 1871. It followed big outbreaks of salmonella food poisoning in Wakefield in August 1984, and of Legionnaires' Disease in Stafford in April 1985. Each provoked a public inquiry. Among its many recommendations was that health authorities appoint a Director of Public Health charged with assessing the health status of the relevant population, and of deriving from this assessment a statement of need.

This brings government policy in line with a more general renaissance in public health, which in recent years has generated public health strategies in many parts of the world. Stemming in part from increasing disillusion with the medical profession, in part from increased concern about environmental health matters, and in part from a switch to individual lifestyle plans which seek to promote health, the public health movement has developed in a climate in which health promotion has become increasingly attractive to the British public, as to others.

British public health strategies can be expected to develop in three main ways.[5] First, the educative function conducted by the Health Education Authority (among others) is likely to increase. Secondly, the increased emphasis on preventive medicine embodied in the GPs' and dentists' contracts implemented in 1990 is likely to provoke a shift from cure to prevention (though the imposition of charges for dental and eye checks in 1989 represented a move in the opposite direction). Thirdly, the idea of healthy public policy is likely to develop through attempts to feed a health dimension into more policy debate, particularly at central government level.

LIMITS TO PUBLIC HEALTH

Health policy should certainly be positive and active. Yet there are limits to its permissible scope. Health policy is only one aspect of our communal lives, and needs inevitably to be traded off with policies which are expressive of other values.

A simple example can be used to illustrate this point. We might agree as a society that smoking is a direct cause of cancer, yet still accept that a total ban on smoking is impermissible because of the constraint on human freedom which would be involved. Indeed, this is the precise trade-off that we do currently make. However, as the public health consequences of smoking become more disturbing, we might decide that infringements on behaviour which has damaging consequences for others might be necessary. Many other examples could be cited.

In these circumstances, it is possible to argue at a very general level that positive action to provide basic health care for all is a prerequisite of a civilised society. Beyond this, however, necessary details can only be filled in by actual societies, each of which is likely to make a different trade-off between competing values. On the one hand, common understandings of basic health require specification. On the other, the sorts of limitations on human conduct which we feel are justifiable on health grounds require detailed assessment.

Should public health initiatives overstep the limits of public support, they are in any case likely to be ineffective. Seat belt laws, which are widely respected in Britain, have had to be repealed in some American states because public observance of them was so slight.

RIGHTS TO HEALTH

Finally, it is worth briefly investigating the notion of a right to health, for it is in many ways central to the debate about access. In the health sphere, what rights do people have?

A clear and influential answer to this question was given by the World Health Organisation when, like the NHS itself, it was established in the aftermath of World War Two. Defining health as 'a state of complete physical, mental and social wellbeing and not merely the absence of disease or infirmity', the WHO affirmed such a state to be 'one of the fundamental rights of every human being'. This maximalist understanding of human rights in the health sphere is an attractive and in many ways compelling stance. It cannot, however, be admitted to the realm of real politics. To declare something a right is to imply that associated obligations can be met. By this criterion, the WHO's declaration is entirely vacuous.

Similar problems infect the prerequisites built into WHO's much-lauded 'Health for All 2000' programme, which are strictly unattainable in this world. 'Without peace, social justice, enough food and safe water, adequate education, decent housing and a useful role in society and an adequate income for every person,' runs the preamble to the programme, 'there can be no health for the people, no real growth and no social development'. Such contributions are of little help in orientating a debate about health.

Instead, rights to health must focus on that which has some possibility of enforcement should set standards fail to be met. Once this condition is established, a right to health itself becomes meaningless. Good health is not a condition which can be guaranteed by any public agency (or any private one for that matter). Only a right to health care can be created with any possibility of enforcement. This is, then, the core notion in terms of which debate must be framed.

THE FUTURE OF ACCESS IN THE NHS

In a mature political society, it seems only right and proper that collective decisions about health care policy should be taken politically. However, limits to explicit rationing must be acknowledged.

On the one hand, it must be recognised that subtle rationing by doctors and other health care professionals will always operate to undermine any explicit rationing criteria which might be developed through public debate. Indeed, all health care systems will always contain elements of paternalism and professional autonomy, for information about individual health care interests will never be sufficiently widespread to allow all people to take for themselves the health care decisions which confront them. On the other, it must be accepted that it could be a long time yet before the British public is ready to take significant responsibility for rationing decisions. For many years to come, we may prefer our existing paternalistic system to continue. Indeed, the nature of the challenge which would face the British people were explicit rationing processes to be introduced in health care should not be under-estimated.

That said, a shift in the direction of public agreement on access criteria seems certain to happen. Before too long we will be forced as a society to establish explicit lists of core and non-core NHS services. Indeed, both North East Thames RHA and Mid Essex DHA (which is in the North East Thames region) have started to exclude some minor treatments – such as varicose vein repair, tattoo removal, excision of lumps and bumps, extraction of wisdom teeth, and 'in vitro' fertilisation – from their lists of permissible NHS treatments.[6] Within a matter of years the British public will find itself enmeshed in rationing debates which will in all probability draw on QALY indices, or their future, more sophisticated equivalents.

This is in many ways a gruesome prospect. Nevertheless, conduct of British health care policy does require more openness, in order that strategic choices which now face the NHS can be informed by public debate. Do we want to increase access to routine (and cheap) rather than glamorous (and expensive) operations, to preventive rather than curative treatments, to the young rather than the old, to those who have taken care of their health (by, for example, not smoking) rather than those who have not? These are key choices. Decisions one way or the other can only properly be made through democratic and participatory procedures. They should not be made uniquely by health care professionals. Equally, they should not simply be left to the interplay of fragmented institutions in a health care market.

NOTES

1. Rationing in Oregon is discussed at length in *Health Affairs* 10,2 (Summer 1991).
2. For a fuller discussion, see D M Fox and H M Leichter, 'Rationing Care in Oregon: The New Accountability', *Health Affairs* 10,2 (Summer 1991), 7-27.
3. R Klein, 'Warning Signals from Oregon', *British Medical Journal* 304 (1992), 1457-8.
4. Secretary of State for Health, *The Health of the Nation: A Consultative Document for Health in England*, Cm 1523 (HMSO, London, 1991).
5. R Baggott, 'Looking Forward to the Past? The Politics of Public Health', *Journal of Social Policy* 20 (1991), 191-213.
6. F Honigsbaum, *Who Shall Live? Who Shall Die? Oregon's Health Financing Proposals* (King's Fund College, London, 1991).

CONCLUSION

Two important reform processes have fed through the NHS in recent years. The first is the paradigm shift to general management which dates, in developed form, from 1984. The second is fragmentation of the NHS embodied in internal market reforms which have been implemented, on a gradualist basis, since 1991. The combined impact of these reform processes on the NHS, and ways in which that impact could be made more positive, have been central concerns of preceding chapters. It remains to review those concerns, and to answer the key question which was posed at the start of this book: will the NHS at the end of the 1990s continue to claim to offer universal health coverage not on the basis of income or advantage, but simply on the basis of need?

THE DRIVE TO REFORM

Many factors explain NHS reform. Among them the roles of chance and circumstance should not be dismissed. In the health sphere, as in all others, government policy is by no means fully coherent. Nevertheless, it is possible to identify a number of dominant themes which have determined the main thrust of NHS reform under successive Conservative governments, even if they have not always been responsible for each of its details.

The drive to reform in the early and mid 1980s was provided by a commitment to business practices in which, it was (correctly) felt, the NHS was sorely lacking. Attempts were therefore made to develop a businesslike orientation within the NHS, and to impose clear managerial hierarchies on the people who worked in it. In this way, the paradigm shift to general management was made. Although it met with often substantial professional resistance, there is no doubt that it succeeded in generating a cultural shift within the NHS. Business structures and practices are now more prevalent in it than was previously the case.

At the end of the 1980s and in the 1990s the drive to reform has been provided by a commitment to quasi-market principles of which, it is (again correctly) felt, the NHS has been largely devoid. In consequence, the NHS has been split into purchaser and provider functions, and a series of contractual relations has been established between the two sides of the new internal market. In the process, parts of the NHS have been encouraged to develop as autonomous units inside the overall NHS structure. Again, it is clear that the impact on NHS operations will eventually be substantial. Within months of institution of the purchaser-provider distinction, key individuals and groups in the NHS were responding to the new market dynamics created by it.

THE CONTEXT OF REFORM

Reform of the NHS has therefore been radical, certainly by previous standards. In the 1970s a substantial restructuring took place, and the Service was disrupted and reordered in many important ways. Yet, significant as the 1974 reorganisation undoubtedly was, it went with the grain of NHS operations in attempting to enhance its ability to deliver a universal and egalitarian health care service through mechanisms of consensus management and strategic planning. Reform in the 1980s and 1990s has had the twin objectives of replacing consensus management, and of undermining strategic planning. In this way it has gone very much against the grain of previous NHS operations, though only in 1991 did the old NHS actually start to be dismantled.

This radicalism makes NHS reform in the 1980s and 1990s seem exceptional. The role of Margaret Thatcher in directing much of it, particularly the internal market programme, heightened public suspicion in the late 1980s that the NHS was being singled out for a notably political restructuring. Yet similar reforms are in fact taking place both in other parts of the British welfare state, and in health care systems in other countries. In each case, the public contract model identified in Chapter 4 is beginning to predominate.

The actual context of NHS reform is not therefore particularly political. It is, instead, a widespread attempt to introduce business principles and market relations to many aspects of (welfare) states the world over.

THE IMPACT OF REFORM

The impact of reform is not entirely positive. Here, most criticism has been directed at excessive fragmentation of the NHS which, it has been argued, threatens to undermine the universalistic and egalitarian impulses which were present in its creation, and which continue to be valued by the British people in the health care sphere even as they are being abandoned in others. Fragmentation of the NHS is the single greatest challenge to its historic attempt to provide universal health coverage on the basis not of income or advantage, but simply of need. There is a real chance that by the end of the present decade core health care distributions will be considerably more diverse than is presently the case. The extreme fragmentation which is most likely to generate this state of affairs is, moreover, unnecessary. The benefits of marketisation can be secured without it.

Yet positive aspects of the reform programme should not be obscured by problems posed by fragmentation. Both the introduction of general management and the more recent marketisation reforms have made substantial progress in placing controls on the key independent power base within the NHS, the medical profession. Indeed, doctors are now under attack from two directions. On the one hand, they face increased government regulation of their activities, backed up by a formidable array of new statistics, such as performance indicators. On the other, they face the discipline of competition in a quasi-market.

In both positive and negative ways, the impact of reform on the NHS is substantial. The NHS is certainly a very different organisation now from what it was when the Conservatives were first elected to office in 1979. It will change still further as the 1990s progress. Yet alongside a picture of constant change, it must again be emphasised that some things – in particular the NHS funding regime – have scarcely changed at all. Other aspects of the NHS – such as conditions of access to it – are only just beginning to register the impact of reform.

THE FUTURE

The future of the NHS is uncertain. The very different dynamics of the managerial and marketisation reforms which are currently feeding through it could interact in many ways to restructure Britain's health care system in the 1990s. It has been argued here that the most likely future for the NHS is a hybrid situation of substantial fragmentation (by means of GP fundholding) in some parts of the internal market, and of increased central direction (by means of the NHS Management Executive in particular) in others. Neither aspect of this scenario is entirely welcome.

Far more desirable is a future which seeks both to build on the advantages of marketisation – notably the choice and responsiveness which it generates – and to offset some of its inherent disadvantages – in particular, the extreme diversity of outcomes which it produces. This future, it has been argued here (in line with the ideas of Enthoven), is attainable through institution of a series of strategic purchasing agencies on the American HMO model.

It has also been argued that NHS funding would be better managed not by the present arrangement of funding out of general taxation, but by a health tax combined with social insurance provisions for those who wish to opt out of public arrangements and contract their own health care cover. A case for increased private payment has also been made. By these means, the NHS might finally be at least partially released from the underfunding debate in which it now seems to be perpetually enveloped.

In the end, however, a better future for the NHS will only be secured by public awareness of its inherent strengths and weaknesses. More funding may well be necessary to a successful NHS future, but it will never be sufficient. In the increasingly developed debates – about access and rationing, to name but two important (and linked) topics – which are certain to feature strongly in the NHS's future, only a clear understanding of its nature, and of ways in which it functions, will enable it to flourish and prosper.

A BRIEF GUIDE TO FURTHER READING

The best (and shortest) recent guide to the health reforms is Chris Ham, *The New National Health Service: Organization and Management* (Radcliffe Medical Press, Oxford, 1991). Valuable for its historical perspective and acute judgment is Rudolf Klein, *The Politics of the National Health Service*, second edition (Longman, London, 1989). Also good in these respects is Ruth Levitt and Andrew Wall, *The Reorganized National Health Service*, fourth edition (Chapman and Hall, London, 1992). Very useful as a source book is Barbara Connah and Ruth Pearson (eds), *NHS Handbook*, seventh edition (NAHAT/Macmillan, London, 1991). Excellent on comparative perspectives is Chris Ham, Ray Robinson and Michaela Benzeval, *Health Check: Health Care Reforms in an International Context* (King's Fund Institute, London, 1990). Comprehensive in its review of public health is Bobbie Jacobson, Alwyn Smith and Margaret Whitehead, *The Nation's Health: A Strategy for the 1990s*, revised edition, (King Edward's Hospital Fund for London, London, 1991).

It is also worth reading the White Papers in which the main lines of health reform are set out. Chief among these are *Promoting Better Health* (Cm 249, November 1987), *Working for Patients* (Cm 555, January 1989) and *Caring for People* (Cm 849, November 1989). Virginia Bottomley's health targets are to be found in *The Health of the Nation: A Strategy for Health in England* (Cm 1986, July 1992). The Acheson Report on public health is officially entitled *Public Health in England* (Cm 289, January 1988).

Journals such as the *British Medical Journal* and the *Health Service Journal* often carry useful articles, and are very good sources of information. The American journal, *Health Affairs*, is also excellent, not simply on America, but on health systems the world over. It is, however, difficult to find in the UK.

INDEX